Swedish Gothic

Anthem Studies in Gothic Literature

Anthem Studies in Gothic Literature incorporates a broad range of titles that undertake rigorous, multi-disciplinary and original scholarship in the domain of Gothic Studies and respond, where possible, to existing classroom/module needs. The series aims to foster innovative international scholarship that interrogates established ideas in this rapidly growing field, to broaden critical and theoretical discussion among scholars and students, and to enhance the nature and availability of existing scholarly resources.

Series Editor
Carol Margaret Davison – University of Windsor, Canada

Swedish Gothic
Landscapes of Untamed Nature

Yvonne Leffler

ANTHEM PRESS

Anthem Press
An imprint of Wimbledon Publishing Company
www.anthempress.com

This edition first published in UK and USA 2023
by ANTHEM PRESS
75–76 Blackfriars Road, London SE1 8HA, UK
or PO Box 9779, London SW19 7ZG, UK
and
244 Madison Ave #116, New York, NY 10016, USA

British Library Cataloguing-in-Publication Data
A catalogue record for this book is available from the British Library.

Library of Congress Control Number: 2022936846
A catalog record for this book has been requested.

ISBN-13: 978-1-83998-0-336 (Pbk)
ISBN-10: 1-83998-0-338 (Pbk)

This title is also available as an e-book.

CONTENTS

An Introduction to Swedish Gothic: History and Works   1

1. The Nordic Wilderness and Its Monstrous Creatures   17

2. The Gender-Coded Landscape and Transgressive Female Monsters   35

3. Nordic Noir and Gothic Crimes   49

4. Swedish Gothic: Dark Forces of the Wilderness   63

Notes   67

List of Swedish Titles Referred to in the Book   73

Bibliography   77

Index   81

AN INTRODUCTION TO SWEDISH GOTHIC: HISTORY AND WORKS

In Sweden from the 1990s onwards, Gothic has invaded all cultural registers – highbrow literature, feature film, popular culture, children's books and young-adult fiction. Furthermore, it has been well received by audiences and critics both inside and outside the country. Most works are produced in response to the international tradition of Gothic with references to international classics and iconic works produced outside Scandinavia. In that way, Swedish Gothic upholds a long domestic tradition of densely intertextual Gothic that goes back to the Romantic period and the beginning of the nineteenth century.

Still, Swedish Gothic is a rather unexplored subject in the field of Gothic studies. One reason for this neglect is the global predominance of the Anglo-American tradition and scholarly studies dedicated to it. Another explanation is the strong realism-prone literary practice in Sweden; Gothic texts with self-conscious unrealism, anxiety-provoking imaginary and a mode of revealing something unconscious or supernatural have not met the requirements as high-brow literature until the late twentieth century. As Rosemary Jackson writes about fantastic art in general, Swedish Gothic has been ignored by native literary critics who have been engaged with 'establishment ideals rather than with subverting them'.[1] It was first in the 1990s that the existence of Gothic fiction was systematically examined in a number of studies by Yvonne Leffler.[2] Since the millennium, scholars such as Mattias Fyhr, Sofia Wijkmark and Henrik Johnsson have studied different writers and aspects of Swedish Gothic. Most of the early studies have been dealing with nineteenth-century literature and canonised writers, such as August Strindberg and Selma Lagerlöf.[3] In the last decades, there has been a growing interest in other cultural forms and Gothic stories in different media, such as film, rock music and young-adult fiction.[4] Drawing on these studies, this chapter will give a survey of Swedish Gothic from the early nineteenth century until the present moment.

The Rise of Swedish Gothic

By the end of the eighteenth century, many of the first English, German and French Gothic novels were imported, available for sale and possible to borrow

from commercial libraries in Sweden. In addition, some of them were quickly
translated into Swedish. For example, Matthew Lewis's *The Monk* (1796) was
published in Swedish in 1800–04. Five novels by Ann Radcliffe were available in Swedish between 1800 and 1806, among them *The Mystery of Udolpho*
(1794) and *The Italian* (1797). The last one was adapted into a play as *Eleonora
Rosalba, eller Ruinerna i Paluzzi* in 1801–03, while François Guillaume Ducray-
Duminil's French novel *Viktor, a Child of the Forest (Viktor, ou l'Enfant de la Forêt,*
1796) was staged as the same theatre in Stockholm – Arsenalen – as *Victor,
eller skogsbarnet* in 1803–04. Although most educated Swedes read literature in
French and German, Ducray-Duminil's 'romans noir' *Viktor, a Child of the Forest*
and *Celina, or the Mystery Child (Coelina, ou l'Enfant du Mystère,* 1798) were printed
in Swedish in 1802–03. Friedrich Schiller's unfinished German ghost story or
Schauerroman, The Ghost-Seer (Der Geisterseher, 1787–89), was published in Swedish
in 1898–1902 and many of E. T. A. Hoffmann's short stories were distributed
in Swedish in the 1820s, such as 'The Magnetiser' ('Der Magnetiseur', 1814)
and 'The Uncanny Guest' ('Der unheimliche Gast', 1819/1821).

The first phase of imported Gothic novels inspired Swedish writers, at the
same time as they domesticated their stories for the local audiences. Although
not choosing a Swedish location as setting, the Romantic poet Erik Johan
Stagnelius contributed to the rise of Swedish Gothic with three plays, which
in handbooks are named *horror dramas (skräckdramer).*[5] In them, he combines
Gothic themes with tormented characters in the tradition of German *Sturm-
und-Drang* dramas, such as Johann Wolfgang Goethe's *Götz von Berlichingen
(Götz von Berlichingen mit der eiseren Hand,* 1773) and Friedrich Schiller's *The
Robbers (Die Räuber,* 1781). Stagnelius's plays *The Prostitute in Rome (Glädje-Flickan
i Rom)* and *Albert and Julia (Albert och Julia),* both first printed in 1825, are
about unhappy love and split characters that lose control of their passions and
because of that they are punished by anxiety, madness, death and damnation. The religious elements from the allegorical morality play are notable, at
the same time as the protagonists' mental conflicts transport them to a world
of nightmare.

Compared to these works, Stagnelius's third play *The Knight's Tower
(Riddartornet,* 1821–23) is a horror drama with a dramatic plot and the use of
dramatic irony to create suspense. It is about Sir Rheinfels, who returns from
war and discovers that his wife has been unfaithful to him. To punish her,
he locks her up in a tower of his castle, at the same time as he makes their
daughter Mathilda believe that her mother is dead. When Mathilda eventually finds out about her imprisoned mother, she asks her father to allow her
to visit her. Rheinfels decides to use the situation in his favour; if Mathilda
marries him, he will release her mother. The drama reaches its climax when
Mathilda, who is plagued by shame and anxiety, is forced to swear to marry

her father, an oath that leads to her death. The suspenseful plot and the changing positions of the conflict-ridden characters generate a Gothic atmosphere. The characters appear to be copies and distorted reflections of each other in an unpredictable and uncanny way. Mathilda and her mother are doubles, at the same time as Rheinfels acts like a distorted version of a patriarch and romantic lover. In addition, some of the minor characters reflect, double and distort the roles of the protagonists in a way that destabilises the distinction between the characters and stresses the themes of destructive romance and incest.

Contrary to Stagnelius, most Romantic prose writers chose Swedish locations as Gothic settings. Clas Livijn's short story, 'A Fantasy of the Conscience' ('Samvetets fantasi', 1821) is a fantastic story in the mode of Hoffmann's fantasies with embedded stories told by several narrative voices. It is set in the Swedish university town of Uppsala. In the frame, two graduated students take farewell at the ruins of the old castle. Before they part, they decide to meet in 30 years at the same place and time. At their reunion at night three decades later, one of them, Erik, conveys a ghastly story about his successful career in the army, and in what way he found out about a former girlfriend's unhappy fate. The main part of the story is about his nightmarish visions of a grey man who haunts him because of the crime he committed when he deserted his girlfriend and, therefore, caused her and their child's death. On the one hand, the grey man can be interpreted as a punishing projection of Erik's bad conscience. On the other hand, Erik tells his friend about his terrifying visions already in the frame of the embedded story, which take place thirty years earlier and before he seduced the girl. In that way, the different narrative perspectives enhance the atmosphere of predestination and the ambiguity of the story. The grey man can both be explained as an image of Erik's scruples and as an indication of a higher spiritual order, because when Erik falls silent, his friend finds him dead.

The First Surge of Gothic Stories

Patriarchal despotism and women as victims in a national setting are recurrent features in Swedish Gothic from the early nineteenth century until the present day. At the same time as the writers employ established Gothic motifs, they transform them to address domestic issues. Carl Jonas Love Almqvist, one of the most recognised Swedish writers, critics and composer in the early and mid-nineteenth century, initiated his literary career with a closet drama, *Amorina* (*Amorina*, 1821). It takes place in a recognisable Swedish setting, outside the capital Stockholm, at the same time as it ridicules certain local traditions and conducts. The female protagonist, the eccentric but charming Amorina appears in a variety of weird situations and she is constantly threatened by male wrongdoers. The most obvious example of Gothic features is the character Johannes, who like a vampire must drink warm blood to survive. Because of his forbidden desire, he lives like an outlaw in the countryside in order to be able to satisfy his needs by killing lambs, which adds a religious dimension to Johannes's vampirism.

In many of Almqvist's later works, unreliable narrators and weird coincidences generate an uncanny atmosphere that remain of Hoffmann's technique of unreliable narration. Two illustrating examples are the novellas, *The Palace* (*Palatset*, 1838) and *Skällnora Mill* (*Skällnora qvarn*, 1838), both of which are structured like a journey into the unknown, a secret and fear-provoking place. In *The Palace*, Almqvist's recurrent first-person narrator, Richard Furumo, tells about his visit to an English seaport and his frightening introduction to Japanese culture. Out of curiosity, Furumo lines up for a ride and ends up in a labyrinthine palace, in which he meets an old Japanese merchant who asks him to assist him to fulfil his dreadful plans. Although it does not end according to the merchant's wish, Furumo leaves both the family and the palace in ashes. Like many Gothic narrators, such as Edgar Allan Poe's narrator in his somewhat later story 'The Fall of the House of Usher' (1839), Furumo's visit to the palace leads him into a world of mystery and terror. Although he manages to escape, he is not able to save the house and its members from total extinction. His main function is to be an eyewitness and to communicate the story.

Also, in Almqvist's *Skällnora Mill*, the anonymous first-person narrator is transported into an unknown world of nightmare where he, in a state of trance-like astonishment, witnesses the planning of cruel acts, which he tries to prevent from happening. However, the narrator-protagonist in *Skällnora Mill* is somewhat more successful than Furumo in *The Palace*. During one of his long-distance walks, he ends up at a mill where he overhears a conversation between the miller and another man about the death of a farmer's wife. In the rest of the story, the narrator tries to find out what happened and to change the course of events by saving a servant girl from being killed. Although the narrator's detective-like approach to the crime makes the story resemble a whodunit-story with a distinct order of unravelling, the unreliability of the narrator enhances the ambiguity of the story and undermines the interpretation of the characters and their actions. The mystery of the dead woman is never solved. What killed her is never convincingly proven and her death remains just as much a mystery when the narrator leaves as when he arrived at the mill.

Finnish-Swede Zacharias Topelius also established a Gothic subgenre of mystery and crime with a Gothic setting and an unreliable first-person narrator. In the frame of 'A Night and a Morning' ('En natt och en morgon', 1843), the first narrator declares he is to retell a senior vicar's story. The embedded first-person narrative starts like many Gothic tales with the narrator's arrival on a stormy night to a gloomy place, a decayed vicarage where the watchdog wails like a wolf while the old housekeeper escorts him to his deceased predecessor's haunted rooms. During the night, he is repeatedly disturbed by ill-omened visions and dreams. In the morning, he is convinced his predecessor was killed and opens an enquiry of a suspected murder case. The meticulous and methodical investigation is constantly obstructed by irrational elements connected to the victim's mentally ill daughter. Like in Almqvist's *Skällnora Mill*, a female character has an ambiguous role; like the servant girl in Almqvist's story, the former vicar's daughter in Topelius' story is both a vulnerable female victim and the core of the mystery. Because Almqvist's and Topelius's male detectives fail to recognise the Gothic pattern of repressed desires, they are unable to crack the code without help. Cold reason and facts are not enough to solve the mystery, nor does reason provide fair justice to the perpetrators and victims.

In the 1840s, several Swedish novelists inserted Gothic crime stories in their novels to complicate and expose the characters' mental conflicts. One of the most successful was Emilie Flygare-Carlén, whose novels were widely disseminated in Europe and the United States.[6] In her breakthrough novel, *The Rose of Tistelön* (*Rosen på Tistelön*, 1842), the plot is based on an authentic murder case found in court records about a smuggler and his oldest son, who killed a custom officer and his crew on a stormy night at sea. They succeeded to keep their crime a secret for many years, but eventually the smuggler's youngest son reported the murder and had his father and brother hanged. Flygare-Carlén's novel opens by describing the night of the crime, and the main plot revolves around how the families of the criminals and their victims are hit by the crime. The detailed description of the slaughter in the beginning of the novel together with the portrayal of the sole witness, the smuggler's weak-minded son, turns the story into a Gothic thriller set in the Swedish archipelago. Although the reader is informed about the crime, most of the characters are ignorant and act accordingly. The main plot is about the smuggler's youngest daughter Gabriella and the murdered custom officer's son Arve and their budding romance. Their love turns the smuggler's mad son into an ominous revenger who threatens to expose the crime whatever methods his father applies to prevent this. His increasingly unpredictable behaviour and ill-omened insinuations change the isle of Tistelön into a Gothic room controlled by a madcap, who believes himself to be *Näcken*, a treacherous water creature known from popular belief. In that way, the power of nature and local myths add to a Gothic atmosphere of predestination and the theme of ancestral sin.

Besides Gothic crime and mystery stories, some writers wrote stories directly in response to international bestsellers. John Polidori's *The Vampire* (1819) inspired Viktor Rydberg to the first Swedish vampire novel *The Vampire* (*Vampyren*, 1848). Rydberg expanded on Polidori's story; he added a subplot about a gang of Italian villains and the portrayals of the vampire and his victims are developed. As Victor Svanberg notes, Rydberg also reused and developed the motif of the vampire in the mode of Théophile Gautier in his latter and best-known novel, *Singoalla* (1857), which he rewrote three times until 1894.[7] Like in Gautier's French tale 'The Dead Woman in Love' ('La morte amoreuse', 1836), Rydberg's *Singoalla* is about a young man torn between love at first sight and his religious Christian duties. It is set in Medieval time and the protagonist is a Swedish crusader, Erland Månesköld, who falls in love with a foreign girl, Singoalla. Although the couple is married by blood oath on a moonlit night according to a ritual used by Singoalla's people, Erland's parents part them and their priest tries to erase Erland's memories of Singoalla by exorcism. However, in the second part of the novel when a young boy arrives and reminds Erland of Singoalla, Erland splits into two personalities, the nocturnal Erland, who is still in love with Singoalla and the diurnal crusader, who is haunted by vague memories of an evil female creature. When the boy at moonlit nights sedates Erland into a somnambulistic stage in order to reunite him with Singoalla, the connotations to vampirism is strengthened. Thus, night, moon and blood are recurring elements connected to Singoalla, at the same time as they achieve a profound symbolic significance that increases the ambiguity of the romance between Erland and Singoalla.

Contrary to most previously published stories, the Gothic genre is given in the titles of two Finnish-Swedish novels – Axel Gabriel Ingelius's, *The Grey Castle* (*Det gråa slottet*, 1851) and Zacharias Topelius's *The Green Chamber at Linnais Mansion* (*Gröna kammarn i Linnais gård*, 1859) – and in Aurora Ljungstedt's *The House of the Devil* (*Hin Ondes hus*, 1853). The three stories are written in the tradition of English explained mystery novels. They revolve around dark family secrets located to haunted houses, passion driven male protagonists and persecuted Gothic heroines. In particular in *The House of the Devil*, a mysterious townhouse in Stockholm with subterranean passages and dreary rooms is depicted with explicit references to Ann Radcliffe's Gothic formula. The dreary rooms and passages are progressively reflecting the dark forces within the inhabitants. In *The House of the Devil*, as well as in *The Grey Castle*, the narrative technique of anticipation, parallels and repetition makes the characters appear forced to repeat the crimes of the ancestors that also motivates the ill-fated endings of the novels. The only novel with a happy conclusion is *The Green Chamber at Linnais Mansion*, in which the mystery of the hauntings is solved when the present owner recognises and reconciles his ancestor's crime and restores the rightful heir to Linnais Mansion. Like in Horace Walpole's *The Castle of Otranto*, Topelius's novel concludes when the true lord is restored on the throne and when he is united with the former owner's daughter.

Fin de Siècle Gothic

By the end of the nineteenth century, the second surge of English-language Gothic reached Sweden; Edgar Alan Poe's short stories, Bram Stoker's *Dracula* (1897), and Robert Louis Stevenson's *The Strange Case of Dr Jekyll and Mr Hyde* (1886) were circulated in Swedish. Other writers with Gothic qualities, such as French Charles Baudelaire, British Oscar Wilde and Joseph Conrad, also influenced Nordic writers. Swedish August Strindberg considered himself a reincarnation of Poe because he was born the same year as Poe died.[8] As Johnsson demonstrates, Strindberg combines several Gothic motifs in his stories and dramas.[9] In his play *Ghost Sonata* (*Spöksonaten*, 1907), the distinction between the dead and the living is blurred and the motif of the doppelganger is fused with that of Nordic *fylgia*, a female creature that is haunting and draining the living of blood and life. Also, in Strindberg's novella *Tschandala* (*Tschandala*, 1888), the protagonist Törner sees his companion Jensen as a parasitic doppelganger and their relationship is depicted as an emotional power struggle, in which Törner tries to eliminate his antagonistic double in order to save his mind. As in many works by Strindberg, the story explores the theme of identity, the battle of minds and, in particular, the fear of loss of male identity and control.

Like other writers of the Modern Breakthrough, that is, the strong movement of naturalism and debating literature in Scandinavia by the end of the nineteenth century, Strindberg used Gothic motifs and narrative technique to highlight a society in crisis. In his satire of Stockholm society *The Red Room* (*Röda rummet*, 1879), the young journalist Arvid Falk finds hypocrisy and political corruption in most social activities. In the end, when he once again meets the mysterious and ever-present Doctor Borg, the novel, as Göran Pintz-Påhlsson claims, turns into a German *Bundesroman*, where the protagonist is secretly watched over and controlled by members of a secret league as part of his education and initiation into the association or society.[10] Thus, Doctor Borg seems to be behind all weird happenings and coincidences Falk experiences. If the novel starts as a political satire on life in contemporary Stockholm, it ends as an uncanny story about a protagonist in the hands of an underground organisation in control of most social activities in the Swedish capital.

By the end of the nineteenth century, women writers used Gothic elements to protest against the predominant gender order. An early example
is Russian-Finnish Marie Linder. In her Swedish-language novel, *A Woman
of Our Time* (*En qvinna af vår tid*, 1867), a Gothic setting and a demonic father
with a dark past expose the subjection of women, domestic violence and wom-
en's exclusion from public life. As Kati Launis argues, the political message
is clear; the horrors in Linder's feminist novel are related to the past, whereas
the heroine Lucy Suffrage's fight for freedom provides hope for a better life
for 'a woman of our time'.[11]

Like Linder, the Nobel laureate Selma Lagerlöf's employed Gothic motifs
and narrative techniques to communicate a feminist message. The most
obvious example is her short story 'The Ghost's Hand' ('Spökhanden', 1898),
where a young woman's fear of the sight of a ghost's hand reflects her fear of
her intended husband and the oppressive mechanism of patriarchy, as Sofia
Wijkmark demonstrates.[12] Also her novel *A Manor House Tale* (*En herrgårdssägen*,
1899) voices a female perspective on a psychological drama, which can be
described as a combination of love story, folk tale and Gothic novel, where the
characters inhabit a borderland between reality and fantasy, sanity and madness, life and death, civilisation and wilderness. In that way, Lagerlöf's stories
are important for the Gothic resurgent at the *fin de siècle*. In most of her fiction,
she moves between romanticism and realism and she often describes complex
mental processes by drawing on motifs of Swedish myths and folktales. In her
episodic novel *Gösta Berling's Saga* (*Gösta Berlings saga*, 1891), a chain of events is
initiated on Christmas Eve, when the 12 *cavaliers* at Ekeby sign a contract with
the Devil, or with his human form or representative, Ironmaster Sintram.
During the coming chaotic year, a series of seemingly supernatural happenings takes place.

Also in many of Lagerlöf's separately published short stories, she explores
various aspects of the return of the past and the relationships between the
human nature and the local landscape, the wilderness. As demonstrated by
Wijkmark, Lagerlöf wrote quite a few short stories that can be seen as *fin de siècle*
Gothic, such as 'The Bloke' ('Karln', 1891), 'The King's Grave' ('Stenkumlet',
1892) and 'Peace on Earth' ('Frid på jorden', 1917).[13] Also one of her most
popular stories 'The Changeling' ('Bortbytingen', 1915) explores the uncanny
relationship between human and untamed represented by a *troll*, as Wijkmark
states.[14] Among Lagerlöf's Gothic stories, the novella *Lord Arne's Silver* (*Herr
Arnes penningar*, 1903) is an expressive example of a murder and ghost story,
where a punishing artic landscape and the Nordic myth of werewolves are
central to the plot. The story set in harsh winter at the Swedish west coast
progresses in short concentrated scenes where the female protagonist's visions
of her dead girlfriend, combined with her lover's shapeshifting nature, give the

story a mythic character. Because of its dramatic composition and technique of anticipation, it could be called the first modern thriller in Swedish literature.[15]

The Rise of Filmmaking in the Interwar Period and Post-War Anxiety

Except for Selma Lagerlöf's fiction, there are few examples of Gothic literature in the early and mid-twentieth century. One of a few examples is Pär Lagerkvist's expressionistic writing in his collection *Evil Tales* (*Onda sagor*, 1924). In his short story 'Father and I' ('Far och jag'), when a boy and his father walk along railway tracks at nightfall, the formerly pastoral landscape becomes eerie when an unscheduled train passes driven by a ghostly figure. Like many of Lagerkvist's early works, an object, the train, which represents modernity and the modern society, provokes anxiety. At the same time, the depiction of the change of the scenery, from rural idyll into expressionistic nightmare, is vital to its Gothic atmosphere.

However, the best examples of Gothic narratives from the 1920s onwards are films. When the art form of cinema emerged, Nordic filmmakers were innovators in creating Gothic atmosphere on the screen, what Fred Botting identifies as *a shadowplay* of light and darkness that characterises the style of *Phantomodernism*.[16] Benjamin Christensen's Swedish-Danish silent film *The Witches* (*Häxan*, 1922) consists partly of documentary-style storytelling about the historical roots and myths of witchcraft and the inquisitors' witch trials in the Middle Ages onwards, partly of dramatised horror sequences where the persecution and execution of women are shown. The explicit notion of the film is that witch hunts stemmed from religious fundamentalism, misogyny and false ideas of the effect of poverty and mental illness that triggered mass hysteria. Because of the graphic depiction of nudity and torture, the film was banned in the United States and it was heavily censored in several other countries. Still, the graphic qualities of the ghostly visualisation of the ride of the witches inspired Walt Disney to illustrate Modest Mussorgsky's orchestral work *Night on Bald Mountain* (*Eine Nacht auf dem Kahlen Berge*) in his animated film *Fantasia* (1940).

Another central movie in the history of Swedish cinema was released at the same time, Victor Sjöström's *The Phantom Carriage* (*Körkarlen*, 1921). The film is famous for its advanced narrative structure with flashback within flashbacks and, in particular, for its technique of double exposure to visualise the world of the dead and to enhance the Gothic qualities of Selma Lagerlöf's novel *The Phantom Carriage* (*Körkarlen*, 1912), on which it is based. The Gothic imagery of Sjöström's film had a major impact on Sweden's most prolific filmmaker Ingmar Bergman. In the film that established Bergman as a world-renowned director, *The Seventh Seal* (*Det sjunde inseglet*, 1957), he utilises the figure of

Death as a *strict master* as an explicit reference to Sjöström's film. Bergman's film, set in Sweden during the Black Death, tells the journey of a medieval knight (Max von Sydow) and his game of chess with the personification of Death (Bengt Ekerot), who has come to take his life. The film has influenced many later directors because of its heavily metaphorical and allegorical style and the way the medieval atmosphere is conveyed by expressionistic lightening, Gothic compositions and viewpoints.

During the post-war anxiety in the mid- and late twentieth century, Gothic tropes and modes of visualisation were frequently exposed in Bergman's films. The claustrophobic setting in the Swedish archipelago and the struggle for power between a nurse Alma (Bibi Andersson) and her traumatised mute patient, the actress Elisabet Vogler (Liv Ullman), turn *Persona* (*Persona*, 1966), into a psychological horror drama. The film plays on the Jungian concept of persona, themes of vampirism and doppelgangers to portray the two women. The usage of mirrors and smoke makes their faces double, dissolve and turn the women into ghostly doubles or different aspects of each other. Therefore, Irving Singer has seen the shot in which the two lookalike faces are combined as an expansion of Stevenson's exploration of duality, the good and evil of human nature in *The Strange Case of Doctor Jekyll and Mr Hyde*.[17]

Referring to the characters in *Persona*, Bergman's *Hour of the Wolf* (*Vargtimmen*, 1968) is even more in the tradition of horror film. It revolves around the disappearance of a painter Johan Borg (Max von Sydow), and according to Bergman, he took inspiration from E.T.A Hoffmann's Gothic novel *The Golden Pot* (*Die goldne Topf*, 1814) and his own nightmares.[18] The film opens when Johan and his pregnant wife Alma (Liv Ullman) arrive at an island to cure his insomnia. Instead of recovery, weird or imagined people plague Johan, and the unreality of John's world intensifies when he and his wife visit an oppressive group of vampire-like aristocrats in their castle. As Lynda Buntzen notes, it is often impossible to distinguish between what is real and what belongs to the painter's hallucinatory world of demons.[19] The surrealistic, near-expressionist style of the film, references to Swedish folk belief about the *hour of the wolf*, and allusions to myths of werewolves and vampires add to the atmosphere of nightmare. In addition, its sparse quiet dialogue accentuates non-human sounds and the claustrophobic atmosphere in a way that, according to José Teodoro, anticipates later seminal horror films, such as Stanley Kubrick's *The Shining* (1980).[20] Like many of Bergman's early films, it applies Gothic tropes and narrative techniques to deal with transgressions of an individual's physical and psychological integrity in both time and space.

The remote artic areas of Scandinavia inspired a number of black-and-white horror films in the mid-twentieth century. Finnish Lapland is the setting in *The White Reindeer* (*Valkoinen peura*, 1952) by Erik Blomberg. The film explores pre-Christian Sami mythology and shamanism and revolves around a young Sami woman (Mirjame Kousmanen). Her visit to a shaman turns her into a shapeshifter, who attracts and kills male herders. Sapmi is also the setting of the American-Swedish science fiction-monster film *Terror in the Midnight Sun (Rymdinvasion i Lappland*, 1959) by Virgil W. Vogel. It screens an alien invasion of the north and a King Kong-like monster attracted to the blond heroine. It starts with two male scientists' investigation of what they first believe to be a meteorite crash but that proves to be an alien spaceship guarded by a hairy biped giant under the control of three humanoid aliens in the spacecraft. After having killed the scientists' staff, torn apart Laplander houses and capturing the heroine, the giant monster meets its tragic end with clear references to the screening of Merian C. Cooper and Ernest Schoedsack's *King Kong* (1933). However, in *Terror in the Midnight Sun*, the artic wilderness and a snowclad cliff replace the urban setting and the Empire-State building of the former film.

International Horror and New Gothic Forms in the Late Twentieth Century

In the 1980s, the global success of horror films inspired Swedish filmmakers to movies, such as Hans Hatwig's *The Bleeder (Blödaren*, 1983), Jonas Cornell's TV drama *The Moon God (Månguden*, 1988), and Joakim Ersgård's *The Visitors (Besökarna*, 1988). Like in earlier films, the Nordic landscape plays a vital role. In *The Bleeder*, a rip off the *Friday the 13th*, the members of an all-girl rock band find themselves trapped in the wilderness when their tour-bus breaks down and they meet an insane beast, whose intention is to kill them off one by one. The killings in the Gothic crime series *The Moon God* are committed in the moonlit forest at nights by a cloaked figure wearing a strange mask. It is for some time unclear if the police chase a supernatural monster or a mentally disturbed serial killer. Also in *The Visitors*, the scenery is significant. Although it is a haunted-house film with explicit references to Stuart Rosenberg's *The Amityville Horror*, the family does not only move into a haunted house but also to a remotely situated house in the Swedish countryside. Like in Kubrick's formative film *The Shining* (1980), Ersgård's film opens with a long shot from above showing the family's car on its way along an empty gravel road in a desolate landscape. Even if the father locates the source of evil to the attic, it seems to be assisted by the landscape. Eventually, the family's only way of escape is to return to town.

From the 1980s onwards and in the tradition of Selma Lagerlöf, women writers started to explore untamed nature and local folklore. In the opening of Kerstin Ekman's Gothic crime story *Blackwater (Händelser vid vatten*, 1993), a violent murder of two campers in the forest is repeatedly described through a series of unreliable sensory impressions and the crime scene is troubling the characters for years to come. Majgull Axelsson's novel *April Witch* (*Aprilhäxan*, 1997) portrays a physically paralysed woman with exceptional mental resources that enable her to take residence in living animals and humans. In that way, she acts like shapeshifters known from Nordic mythology in her quest for justification. In many of Birgitta Trotzig's stories, dark forces invade the human mind. Her novel *The Mud-King's Daughter* (*Dykungens dotter*, 1985) refers to H.C. Andersen's *The Mud-King's daughter* (*Dund-kongens datter*, 1858) and the Brothers Grimm's *The Frog King or Iron Heinrich*, in a story about the transformation of the human body.

In addition to these writers, Mare Kandre's novel *Bübin's Offspring* (*Bübins unge*, 1987), *Aliide, Aliide* (*Aliide, Aliide*, 1991), and *Bestiarium* (1999) are expressing an atmosphere of decay and doom. In them, the scenery enriches the portrayals of the female characters with a symbolic and mythic significance. In *Bübin's Offspring*, the untamed nature of a garden mirrors the psychological development of a pubescent girl, while in *Aliide, Aliide*, the bleak and labyrinthine cityscape corresponds to the mind of an eight-year-old girl.[21] In the same tradition of Gothic are Maria Gripe's books for children and young adults. Her five books in *The Shadow Series* (*Skuggserie*, 1982–88) are suffused with Gothic elements, symbols and Jungian archetypes, in particular the concept of the shadow. As demonstrated by Carina Lidström, the two protagonist's process of development can be described as a quest for identity, where mirroring and metamorphosis are central motifs.[22]

Since the late 1960s, many works for children and young adult included Gothic elements. Two early examples are Leif Krantz's TV series *The Kullen Man* (*Kullamannen*, 1967) and *Crows' Gold* (*Kråkguldet*, 1969). In the first one, four young cousins on summer vacation at the rocky and forested peninsula of Kullaberg are dragged into a dangerous spy drama. In the second one, set just before Christmas in a small mining community, a boy finds a gold nugget and because of his find, local acquaintances and mysterious strangers pursue him. In both series, the local scenery and its myths about ominous men – *Kullamannen* and *Skarp-Erik* – add to the eerie atmosphere. The recurrent shots from the flashing lighthouse och the formations of the cliffs in twilight in *The Kullen Man* and the snowclad woodlands and the ruined headframe surrounded by black crows in *Crows' Gold* accentuate the importance of the location and its sinister past.

At the same time as these TV series for children were broadcasted, a group of writers produced semi-pulp book series, for example, *Cold Chills* (*Kalla kårar*, 1971–84). The series consisted of a number of translated foreign-language stories by, for example, Richard Matheson and John Wyndham, together with Swedish stories by writers, such as Gunnar Dahl and Dagmar

Danielsson. Other important contributions to the Gothic revival were Helmer Linderholm's collection of Swedish short stories *The Wolfish Grey* (*De ulvgrå*, 1972) and Åke Ohlmarks's, *Revenants* (*Gengångare*, 1971) and *Castle Ghosts* (*Slottsspöken*, 1973). While Linderholm's book has a fictional frame about a provincial general practitioner and his wife, whose background in northern Sweden and Finland provides her with a strange ability to handle challenges from powers and beings of Nordic mythology, Ohlmarks's books consist of ghost stories located to various places and castles in Sweden.

The Gothic Revival at the Millennium

In contemporary Swedish Gothic, the plot is often structured as a journey into the unknown, a hostile place beyond pre-conceived conceptions of time and space. In Michael Hjorth's film *The Unknown* (*Det okända*, 2000), a group of young scientists are sent off to investigate a remote fire-ravaged area in northern Sweden where they find themselves increasingly threatened by an alien force of nature. Myrick and Sánchez's *The Blair Witch Project* inspired the film, but in Hjorth's version, there is no witch or identified monster to trace and fight. Instead, the forest acts as a living organism, an uncanny and hostile enemy. Also Sonny Laguna and Tommy Wiklund's *Wither* (*Vittra*, 2012) is about a group of young people and their frightening encounter with the northern woodlands, in this case in form of a *vittra*, an invisible creature from Swedish folklore that lives underground. In the film, some friends organise a weekend trip to a remote cabin. What they do not know is that a *vittra* dwells in the cellar and immediately starts attacking them and turns their holiday into an experience of violence ruled by something barbaric connected to paganism and untamed nature. This theme of modern city-dwellers' encounter with pre-Christian rituals and pagan nature beings is also explored in Anders Fager's *Collected Swedish Cults* (*Samlade svenska kulter*, 2011), a collection of horror stories that are related to each other in an uncanny way and also appear in his role-play *Collected Swedish Cults* (2014).

Gothic conventions and references to American films are used in various horror comedies. Anders Jacobsson's slasher parody and satire towards the censorship of the Swedish Cinema bureau, *Evil Ed* (1995), follows a film editor who goes insane and indulges in messy killings after editing too many gory splatter films. The references to Raimi's *The Evil Dead* are many and noteworthy. Anders Banke's *Frostbite* (*Frostbiten*, 2006) – in the tradition of Roman Polanski's *The Fearless Vampire Killers* – is a playful mockery of vampire films. It is set in northern Sweden during midwinter, making the dark endless winter night the perfect environment for vampires, at the same time as the master vampire operates from the hospital as a geneticist that works on mutations in blood samples. Like in *Evil Ed*, the use of explicit references to well-known international horror films, visual humour and special effects contribute to the parody in *Frostbite*.

As demonstrated in many studies, the Gothic revival is especially noticeable in today's fiction for young adults, in particular in stories about a group of young female witches operating as a collective protagonist in a distinct cultural and social Nordic context.[23] Two illustrative examples are Mats Strandberg and Sara B. Elfgren's bestselling Engelsfors trilogy – *The Circle* (*Cirkeln*, 2011), *Fire* (*Eld*, 2012) and *The Key* (*Nyckeln*, 2013) – and Madeleine Bäck's Gästrikland trilogy: *The Water Draws* (*Vattnet drar*, 2015), *The Soil Arouses* (*Jorden vaknar*, 2017) and *The Mountain Sacrifices* (*Berget offrar*, 2018). In both series, a group of young people develop supernatural abilities in order to fight those evil demons that are taking over the forests surrounding their small mining communities in the Swedish *rust belt*. As in many other stories for young female readers, such as Caroline L. Jensen's *Wolf Kindred* (*Vargsläkte*, 2011), the witches in the trilogy must learn to be responsible and capable of cooperation and to set aside their own interests for the good of others. Thereby, the young heroines in these stories are encouraged to adopt traditional female virtues, such as empathy, in order to support the welfare of other living beings, and the stories describe a utopian matriarchal world where women are in charge and set the rules. They are about girl power and in what way it may save the world, or at least those things worth fighting for or protecting for coming generations.

The true return of Gothic to mainstream culture was John Ajvide Lindqvist's vampire novel, *Let the Right One In* (*Låt den rätte komma in*, 2004). It was quickly translated into many languages and it was adapted into two films: a Swedish-language film directed by Tomas Alfredson in 2008, and an American remake, *Let Me In*, by Matt Reeves in 2010. Like Lindqvist's later stories, such as his zombie novel *Handling the Undead* (*Hanteringen av odöda*, 2005), troll story *Border* (*Gräns*, 2006) and ghost thriller *Harbour* (*Människohamn*, 2008), it illustrates one of the most predominate tendencies in today's Swedish Gothic, a combination of Gothic and social realism. Lindqvist uses supernatural elements and Gothic themes to confront and contest established ideas of the Swedish welfare state. His successful version of everyday reality and Gothic has paved the way for several other novels, such as Mats Strandberg's *Blood Cruise* (*Färjan*, 2015) and *The Home* (*Hemmet*, 2017). In Lindqvist's and Strandberg's works, as Sofia Wijkmark demonstrates, the writers recurrently dismantles the concept of the Swedish *folkhem*, meaning 'the people's home', a metaphorical concept established in the 1930s by the Swedish Social Democratic Party to describe a society of modernity and rationality, where all people were treated as equals and as part of a collective welfare system.[24] In Lindqvists's and Strandberg's novels, supposedly safe places in the well-organised Swedish society become uncanny rooms of alienation and terror. For example, in Strandberg's stories, places that represent vacation or professional care, such as cruise ships or nursing homes for the elderly, become dwellings of supernatural beings and violent death. More openly than Lindqvist's fiction, Strandberg's novels end in horror without any hope of escaping or defeating the evil.

Several works at the millennium explore the same Gothic terrain as earlier stories, namely the wilderness. A recognisable Nordic setting combined with creatures from local mythology serve as a source of inspiration for today's Nordic game developers, such as in Swedish *Year Walk* (2013). However, as Johan Högberg argues, the concept of a regional version of Gothic is questionable in this kind of global games as they are produced for a global market in English.[25] More undisputable examples of Swedish Gothic are stories targeting domestic readers in order to explore local traditions and issues of minorities and climate change. For example, at the beginning of the new century, a number of Swedish writers employed Gothic strategies to tell stories about Sápmi and supernatural agencies rooted in Sámi myths and religious practice, such as Matthias Hagberg's novel *Requiem for a Disable* (*Rekviem för en vanskapt*, 2012), Stefan Spjut's *Stallo* (*Stallo*, 2012) and *Stalpi* (*Stalpi*, 2017). In particular, Spjut's series is an example of generic hybridity, EcoGothic and what Sofia Wijkmark calls *troll fiction*.[26] The first novel opens as a detective story with the disappearance of a little boy but the search for the boy results in the appearance of strange creatures reminding of trolls and shapeshifters known from Nordic folklore and Sámi myths. In Spjut's novels, the trolls pose a significant danger to the human protagonists, at the same time as they represent a species dying due to the expansion of human civilisation.

The last decades have given rise to a surge of internationally well-received Nordic crime stories, so-called Nordic Noir. Some of these stories mix crime and Gothic where the modern crime investigation is obstructed by seemingly supernatural elements. One of the most prolific writers are Johan Theorin and his four novels set on the Swedish Island of Öland, the so-called Öland-quartet: *Echoes from the Dead* (*Skumtimmen*, 2007), *The Darkest Room* (*Nattfåk*, 2008), *The Quarry* (*Blodläge*, 2010), and *The Voices Beyond* (*Rörgast*, 2013). Another writer of Gothic crime set in Sámpi is Cecilia Ekbäck with her two novels set at the fictitious place Blackåsen Mountain: *Wolf Winter* (*I vargavinterns land*, 2015) and *In the Month of the Midnight Sun* (*Midnattssolens timme*, 2016). Also TV series, such as Henrik Björn' *Soil Sprouts* (*Jordskott*, 2015), Thomas Tivemark's *Ängelby* (*Ängelby*, 2015) and Måns Mårlind and Björn Stein's *Midnight Sun* (*Midnattssol*, 2016), are uncanny crime stories located on the outskirts of modern civilisation, in areas that compromise the ideals of today's modern industrialised and urban Swedish society.

Outline of Chapters

As demonstrated above, Swedish Gothic is a highly place-focused version of Gothic, in which the Nordic landscape plays a central part and can be equated with a character in its own right. The Gothic terror is located in the Nordic wilderness and the monstrous *other* is often represented by nature beings from old myths, regional folklore and popular belief. The following three chapters explore three different aspects of the significance of the setting and in what way the Nordic landscape and its creatures are employed to enhance the Gothic atmosphere in Swedish literature, film and TV drama. Each chapter starts with an introductory historical contextualisation exemplified by some early seminal works in Swedish Gothic. The main part of the chapter investigates the occurrence of the same place-focused motifs and themes in representative stories produced after the millennium and in what way they are developed and used to address current topics.

The next chapter, that is Chapter 1, explores the Gothic qualities of the local Swedish setting and in what way Swedish protagonist become victims of the environment, that is, the Nordic wilderness. The second part of the chapter examines the phenomenon of Nordic *troll fiction* and in what way the portrayal of *trolls*, well-known creatures in Swedish lore, can be understood in relation to the concepts of EcoGothic.

The following chapter, Chapter 2, expands on gendered wilderness. In the first part, it demonstrates how stories by male writers and directors work in a tradition of feminised wilderness populated with devious female creatures. The second part of the chapter, explores women writers' use of Gothic elements and female creatures from popular belief, in particular witches as nature beings to address gender issues.

Chapter 3 deals with the boom of Nordic crimes stories since the millennium and the evolvement of a Gothic version of crime fiction, here called Gothic Crime. The main object of this chapter is to explore the distinct features of contemporary Gothic crime and in what way the modern crime investigation is obstructed by seemingly supernatural powers connected to pre-Christian beliefs. The chapter also demonstrate the central position of the setting in Gothic crime and the use of local myths of supernatural powers to activate repressed memories of a dark period in Swedish history in order to address postcolonial issues about environmental exploitation, colonisation and racism.

Finally, Chapter 4 concludes by summarising the most distinct features of Swedish Gothic since the early nineteenth century until present. It also demonstrates the most significant changes over time with focus on the role of the Nordic landscape, the wilderness and the mythological creatures of nature.

Chapter 1

THE NORDIC WILDERNESS AND ITS MONSTROUS CREATURES

Since the early nineteenth century until the present day, Swedish Gothic is set in the Nordic landscape, often in the vast, dark forest, the snow-covered artic fells in the northern part of the country or on a remote wintry island in the archipelago in the Baltic Sea or the west coast of Sweden. The Gothic terror is located in untamed nature and in that kind of environments that Yi-Fu Tuan calls, the *landscapes of fear*, wild and uncontrollable nature beyond the human domain.[1] From the human perspective of environmental experience, Tuan makes a distinction between *place and space*, where place refers to a location filled with human meaning, while space is an abstract concept and a site void of social significance. If place embodies enclosure, security and stability, space represents movement as well as freedom and threat.[2] In addition, regional folklore and old local tradition are employed to enhance the Gothic atmosphere, and the protagonist's dark side is often bound to or triggered by untamed nature and the pagan pre-Christian past of the region. Thus, Swedish Gothic is a place-focused, or topofocal, version of Gothic, in which the landscape plays a central role and can be equated with a character in its own right.

An early example of the vital role of the setting is Emilie Flygare-Carlén's *The Rose of Tistelön* (*Rosen på Tistelön*, 1842) and Victor Rydberg's *Singoalla* (*Singoalla*, 1857) set in the harsh archipelago on the west coast and in the forest land in central Sweden respectively. By the end of the century, Selma Lagerlöf developed this tradition even further in her use of the Nordic wilderness and its local myths in order to explore the characters' repressed desires by drawing on regional folktales and folkloristic motifs in novels such as *Gösta Berling's Saga* (*Gösta Berlings saga*, 1891) and *Lord Arne's Silver* (*Herr Arnes penningar*, 1903). Also, in some of Ingmar Bergman's most formative films, for example, *The Seventh Seal* (*Det sjunde inseglet*, 1957) and *Hour of the Wolf* (*Vargtimmen*, 1968), the scenery – and the characters' place in it – is crucial to the Gothic imagery and the characteristic metaphorical and explorative qualities of Bergman's films.

Since the millennium, untamed nature and its mythical creatures have an even more prominent part in for example Michael Hjorth's film *The Unknown* (*Det okända*, 2000), Sonny Laguna and Tommy Wiklund's film *Wither* (*Vittra*, 2012) and the Swedish computer game *Year Walk* (2013). In addition, the terrifying unknown is repeatedly linked to ancient pre-Christian nature worship in novels such as John Ajvide Lindqvist's *Harbour* (*Människohamn*, 2008).

Furthermore, in recent years, a subcategory of Gothic stories has appeared that revolve around a figure from Nordic myths and folktales, *trolls*. Local myths about trolls, changelings and enchantment have a long tradition. According to popular belief, trolls are a hideous mixture of human and beast, and they are known to be stupid, greedy and unpredictable creatures that live in ancient forests and remote mountains. As voracious predators, they pose a threat to humans, especially Christians. At the same time, they are attracted to human infants that they are inclined to kidnap and keep prisoners in their caves, where they also keep their collected treasures of gold, silver and gems. One of the first to employ troll mythology to explore the dark sides of human nature was Selma Lagerlöf in her collection of stories *Troll and Humans* (*Troll och människor*, 1915). Since the millennium, trolls and changelings have become so popular that Sofia Wijkmark has named this new trend *Nordic troll Gothic*. Some illustrative examples are Charlotte Wize's Danish short story 'Changeling (Skifting, 1996)', Johanna Sinisalo's Finnish novel *Not Before Sundown* (*Ennen päivänlaskaua ei voi*, 2000) and André Øvredal's Norwegian film *Trollhunter* (*Trolljegeren*, 2010).[3] Some specific Swedish examples are Henrik Björn's TV-production *Soil Sprouts* (*Jordskott*, 2015), Stefan Spjut's novels *Stallo* (2012) and *Stalpi* (2017) and John Ajvide Lindqvist's novella *Border* (*Gräns*, 2006), together with Ali Abassi's film adaptation of Lindqvist's story as *Border* in 2018. However, before returning to Spjut's and Ajvide Lindqvist's troll fiction, I will expand on the significance of the Nordic landscape and its dark forces linked to pre-Christian and pagan ideas in Swedish Gothic in two representative novels, Selma Lagerlöf's *Lord Arne's Silver* from the *fin de siècle* and John Ajvide Lindqvist's *Harbour* from the early twenty-first century. Both novels are set in the archipelago and revolve around crime and punishment. In both novels, the local waterscape plays a significant part as the monstrous other.

The Frozen Archipelago of Marstrand

Selma Lagerlöf is one of the most influential writers of place-focused Gothic in Swedish literature. In her novella *Lord Arne's Silver*, the wintry landscape on the Swedish West Coast is a protagonist in its own right. In addition, two mythological Nordic figures are fundamental to the plot, the werewolf and the vengeance-seeking Nordic *gengångare* or revenant. The story is a thrilling murder and ghost story about crime and punishment, love and duty set in an ill-fated Gothic world. Like most ghost stories, according to Julia Briggs' definition, the tension is between certainty and doubt and the main motive is revenge.[4] It is set in the sixteenth century and the story progresses in short concentrated scenes in the style of the Icelandic saga. It opens when the fishmonger Torarin drives his horse and sleigh through a desolate wintry landscape on his way to the wealthy clergyman Lord Arne at Solberga parsonage. When he approaches the farm, his clairvoyant dog howls like a wolf and refuses to accompany him into the yard. During his visit, Torarin recalls that Lord Arne's silver treasure is said to be cursed, at the same time as the deaf old lady of the house is annoyed by the sound of knives being sharpened at a nearby farm. Later the same night, the parsonage is set on fire, the residents are found slaughtered and the chest with silver is missing. By that, the old monks' prophesy that the silver treasure would bring Lord Arne misfortune seems to be fulfilled.

The following course of events is just as doomed. After the massacre, Torarin revisits the burnt-down parsonage and meets the ghosts of the victims, who ask him for retribution. However, it is not Torarin but the sole survivor, the young girl Elsalill that is summoned by her killed friend and foster sister, Sir Arne's granddaughter, to carry out their revenge. The dead girl appears as a resourceful revenant that not only seeks retribution for herself and her dead relatives but also has the means to pull a living person into the project. Recurrently she haunts Elsalill, who after her move to the port of Marstrand has fallen in love with the elegant Scottish mercenary Sir Archie. He and his two companions are trapped in Marstrand by the harsh winter conditions and waiting for the ice to break to be able to set sails for Scotland. Every time Elsalill sees Sir Archie, her dead friend interferes. The revenant makes Elsalill see a loop of fair hair around her lover's hand, in the same way as she saw her dead friend's hair around the hand of her killer. When Sir Archie's friends escort her to meet him, she sees Lord Arne's silver coins rolling in front of her feet. Another time, she observes the ghost whispering in Sir Archie's ear, which makes him and his friends confess their crime as Lord Arne's killers. Because she hesitates to report them to the town guards, she later hears her dead foster sister weeping during the service, and on her way back home from church, she sees the dead girl's bloody footprints in the snow. Thereby, Elsalill is finally convinced that she must betray her lover and his friends; her duty is to see that justice is done. However, by assisting the ghosts to receive retribution, she sacrifices her own life and happiness. Thus, she is the ultimate victim in the story; she is haunted to death by her former bosom friend, Lord Arne's dead granddaughter.

Elsalill's burden is not only that she loves a murderer; she is also in love with a beast, a shapeshifting werewolf, or 'a wolf in the forest' as she concludes in the end.[5] During the investigation of the crime, the massacre appears to be the deed of creatures with supernatural powers. The day before the bloodbath, three journeyman tanners are said to have arrived to a nearby farm, and, according to the farmer's wife, they looked dreadful and like werewolves when they sharpened their 'long knives'.[6] After the slaughter, one of the victims, the fatally wounded curate, claims that the three killers climbed in through a chimney hole in the roof, and they were dressed in shaggy furs and acted like beasts. Furthermore, their footprints left in the snow were made by iron-made shoes or shoed hooves before all traces mysteriously disappeared into a hole in the ice. Later, when the traumatised Elsalill meets Sir Archie in Marstrand, his dual nature of elegant nobleman and slaying wolf is progressively proven to the reader. When she tells her story of 'blood and murder', he and his friends' 'ears grew long with listening, and their eyes glinted, and their lips sometimes parted to show the rows of teeth within' and Sir Archie is described to have 'eyes and teeth of a wolf'.[7] His relationship with Elsalill accentuates his bipolar nature of tender remorseful lover and cunning criminal who denies his former wrongdoings. Because one of his murdered victims, the dead girl, constantly haunts and torments him, he looks upon Elsalill as his redeemer, whose love will liberate him. However, their love story is right from the beginning doomed because orphaned Elsalill cannot resist the will of the ghosts and her duty to her dead foster family. Thereby, she does not only send Sir Archie to the wheel but also to eternal damnation. In the end, when she finally refuses him, it is described how he is taken over by his predatory wolf nature, not sparing anything or anyone in order to escape his punishment. When the town guards arrive to seize him and his companions, he uses Elsalill's body as a shield to help him escape to the frozen-in ship.

In *Lord Arne's Silver*, the theme of crime and punishment is closely linked to the Nordic scenery and climate. The massacre takes place a dusky winter evening and the culprits appear in the shapes of the most feared local predator in winter, the wolf. If Sir Archie and his men are disguised as wolves or actually are transformed into werewolves in the act of killing – and every time they are reminded of it – is never clarified. When they first appear as three journeyman tanners at the farm close to Solberga, they have been lost in the forest for a whole week. Restored by food and drink they transform and look so dreadful that they are believed to be werewolves, a supernatural creature of wilderness. When they act in the shapes of wolves, the season and the frozen landscape trigger and facilitate their deed and escape. However, after the carnage, when the focus of the narrative is on the quest to unmask and catch the killers, the landscape and the powers of nature are progressively intervening into the actions to prevent the evildoers from escaping. The reader is recurrently reminded of the exceptionally harsh conditions of this specific winter. The local landscape seems to cooperate with the ghosts in their project of seeking revenge by keeping all ships frozen-in until the assassins are caught. The day the dead girl finally convinces Elsalill about Sir Archie guilt, a fierce storm roars as if to accompany Elsalill's mental anguish and to tell everybody else in town that now the ice might eventually break to release the frozen-in ships. When she nevertheless decides to go with Sir Archie to Scotland, the storm dies, as if to stop the ice from breaking. Although the port of Marstrand is open, the ship carrying the Scotsmen remains trapped until the skipper hands over the three tied-up murderers to the fishmonger Torarin as well as Elsalill's dead body to the women of Marstrand. At that moment, the cold finally loses its grip and the vessel relieved of its three bloodstained passengers is given free passage to Scotland.

By this means, the intervention of the supernatural forces of nature also has religious implications in Lagerlöf's story. At first, the wintry climate and the frozen ocean facilitate the massacre on Lord Arne and his family as a divine retribution for the fact that his treasure of silver came from robbing monasteries during the time of reformation. Later, the same powers of nature prevent the offenders from escaping with the silver by keeping their ship frozen-in. It is not until Lord Arne's silver is shared among the Scottish soldiers that assisted in catching the murderers that the ice breaks and a condition of normality is re-established in the archipelago outside Marstrand.

The Hostile Baltic Sea at Domarö

Like *Lord Arne's Silver*, John Ajvide Lindqvist's *Harbour* is a crime story that opens a cold wintry day in the archipelago. However, it is more clearly structured as a journey away from ordinary everyday life into a remote alien space representing untamed nature, where the island of Domarö in the Baltic Sea north of Stockholm transforms into a vicious claustrophobic place. The story revolves around Anders's parental anguish and search for his six-year-old daughter Maja, who mysteriously disappeared when he and his wife took her on an excursion to a lighthouse in the middle of the frozen channel outside Domarö. While the parents were inside the lighthouse, Maja ran outdoors and vanished without leaving any traces. Two years later, alone and more or less permanently drunk, Anders returns to the island to recover and come to terms with his loss. Although he is born and bred at Domarö, he realises that people are not telling him all they know about what might have happened; even his grandmother Anna-Greta keeps secrets about the inhabitants and the history of the island.

Anders' homecoming illustrates what William Patrick Day calls 'the theme of descent' and 'a fable of identity fragmented and destroyed beyond repair'.[8] By returning to the island where he once grew up and where he lost his daughter, he moves from the natural world of rational modernity into an underworld of mystery and terror. Although he is in search of his lost daughter, his quest for truth and meaning unsecures the very concept of a continuous human identity. From Anders's viewpoint, the reader is confronted with a number of strange and seemingly supernatural experiences. Anders is haunted by the eerie presence of his daughter and he finds himself more and more forced to act as his daughter used to do; he reads her old Bamsy comics, sleeps in her bed and designs mosaics of her plastic beads. At the same time, a number of other weird activities disturb him and the islanders: a house is mysteriously set on fire, islanders that are believed to be long dead are observed, an almost intact dead body of a woman, who is thought to have drowned many years ago, is washed up on the beach. Furthermore, Anders's old schoolmate, a former beauty queen, has plastic surgery to look uglier, or to look like a woman who lived at the island a century ago. Anders also witnesses his neighbours, who are known to be friends, start attacking each other without any obvious reason. Gradually, he and his grandmother's immigrated partner Simon, a formerly renowned magician, realise that they, just like the other long-time residents at Domarö, are influenced by something in the local environment, probably something connected to the sea.

Although the horror in the novel centres on the recent past and Anders's memories of a traumatic event, the ultimate cause of what occurs in the present time of narration is related to the pagan history of Domarö, a history that is gradually revealed in the novel. According to old sources, the locals once made a pact with the sea; they ensured their livelihood by regular human offerings at the cliff of the lighthouse where Maja disappeared. Although no ritual sacrifices take place any longer, islanders strangely disappear or do not return from a voyage as if the sea regularly takes its tribute. The contract also means, according to Anders' grandmother, that inborn residents are unable to move from the island. However, recently the conditions of the agreement appear to have changed and, according to Simon's conclusion, the sea appears to have grown weaker or more vulnerable.

In the novel, different explanations are given to what might have caused the change at Domarö. Some of them highlight a conflict between nature and culture that adds an environmental dimension to the story. On the one hand, the local residents voice their opposition to the commercial exploitation of the archipelago and wealthy city-dwellers' colonisation of the island by buying up properties; the locals see summer guests and tourists as intruders that change and threaten traditional life by transforming fishing villages into tourist camps. On the other hand, the introduction of modern urban life also causes environmental changes that open up for a more explicit ecological reading. The sea appears endangered by growing human activities and therefore fights back by preying on certain islanders, namely, those known to be socially dysfunctional, aggressive and wicked persons. Therefore, the sea – or a monstrous entity residing in the sea – has expanded its impact by using new methods to get at the islanders as a collective. The most potent one is salt-water intrusion. By contaminating the drinking water, the islanders and their minds are literally invaded by the sea. Under the influence of seawater, the residents start fighting their neighbours or in other ways to offer themselves to the sea.

In that way, the local landscape transforms into a labyrinthine waterscape influencing and influenced by humans. Progressively, the unspecified entity of the sea directs the characters' attention and actions; it communicates by giving rise to visions and it evokes the characters', in particular Anders', repressed memories. At the same time as Anders' search for Maja brings forth the secrets of the island's pagan past, he becomes inherent in the island's history and the sea as such. Under the influence of the contaminated drinking water, his loss and search for truth disturbs his normal perception and distorts his concept of time and space. When he grasps that influenced by Maja's spirit, he has completed a mosaic in the shape of a nautical chart of the archipelago where the rock and the lighthouse is marked in red, he returns to the lighthouse. Equipped with Simon's *Spiritus*, which can be used to control water, he descends into the sea to find Maja. During his submarine visit, he believes himself to be reunited with his daughter, as well as with the past of the island and the sea. He experiences the existence as an intricate web of relations between the living and the non-living, the human and non-human, the human self and nature. To Anders the normal order of time and pace does not exist; everything seems to be meshed in an eternal mythic moment.

Like in *Lord Arne's Silver*, the theme of crime and punishment in *Harbour* is explored from the guilt-ridden victim's viewpoint, in this case Anders, who blames himself for the disappearance of his daughter. At first Anders is that kind of haunted male protagonist Kate Fergusson Ellis finds typical of masculine Gothic; a man exiled from home and earthly happiness.[9] However, unlike in Ellis's masculine Gothic, it is not only a person but also a place that is haunted; in *Harbour* the person is possessed by the haunted place. What first looks as a mysterious kidnapping turns out to be part of a collective punishment originating in a pagan pact. Although Anders struggles to alleviate his parental anguish by searching for Maja, the result of his pursuit of reunion with his daughter is ambiguous. When Anders ascends from the submarine underworld beneath the lighthouse with Maja on his back, he finds himself in a distorted copy of the archipelago where no sounds are heard and the islanders he approaches do not notice him. From his internal viewpoint, the reader enters into a realm of death or hallucination, or maybe Anders experience of being possessed by Maja, or whatever remains of her. In the end, he brings Maja back to the lighthouse to repeat his visit to the submarine underworld in order to return to the world of the living. However, the reader is left in uncertainty of the outcome of his endeavours. Therefore, the ending of the novel is far from clear or happy, where good triumphs over evil, as Henrik Johnsson erroneously claims.[10] The reader does not know if Anders will return and bring Maja to life, or if his search for Maja has made him one more victim of the sea. As gradually exposed, and explicitly expressed by Simon in the end of the novel, Maja was not a normal child; she was aggressive and violent. She was exactly that kind of person the sea takes as a tribute. By birth, she was destined to be taken by the sea or to assist the sea in consuming other native islanders, such as Anders.

The Swedish title of the novel, *Människohamn*, means in Swedish to appear in the form or shape of a human. Thereby it empathises the theme of possession, the ability of something unhuman – such as a sea entity – to take control of the islanders or to act in the shape of those that are already taken, such as the revenants of the bullies Henrik and Björn that returns to haunt Anders. However, the most explicit case of possession is Maja's return to control Anders and make him return to the submarine staircase outside the lighthouse, at the same time as he sees how Domarö is flooded by a tsunami. In the end of the novel, the settlement on Domarö is demolished and the island is literally speaking taken over by the sea. If the sea or its residing entity is appeased by the tribute, in combination with the return of Anders and Maja to the cliff of Gåvosten (Gift Stone or Offering Rock), is left in obscurity. However, when the novel closes, Judgement Day seems to have come and ended life on Domarö, or Judge Island as the Swedish name means.

Troll Mythology at the *Fin de Siècle* and Today

The importance of the Nordic landscape as a realm of fear inhabited by devious creatures known from ancient tales and popular belief is even more developed in today's troll fiction. When Selma Lagerlöf at the *fin de siècle* made use of Nordic troll mythology, it was to explore the uncanny relationship between human and nature, civilisation and wilderness. In her short story 'The Changeling' ('Bortbytingen', 1915), a troll woman steals a farmer's son and leaves her own son in its place. Despite his beastly features and aggressive behaviour, the farmer's wife nurses the troll child and is rewarded for her care when her son is returned to her. In another story, 'Peace on Earth' ('Frid på jorden', 1917), Lagerlöf explores another idea connected to trolls, the myth of *bergtagning*, literally meaning to be taken by or into the mountain. It means either to be trapped in the mountain or to be put under a spell or spirited way into the mountains by the trolls, or other supernatural nature beings. If the imprisoned persons ever return, they have changed into another personality and have lost their souls. In Lagerlöf's story that takes place at Christmas, a family is visited by a frightening ghostly figure that is later recognised as a missing daughter who once disappeared in the woods never to be found by her family. The return of the abused and violated woman turns the family's Christmas celebration into a time of terror and guilt. As Sofia Wijkmark claims, the story proves the working of Freud's concept *das Unheimliche*, the return of something repressed and familiar; the woman transforms the home – including the family members – into an unhomely and uncanny place.[11] It also shows in what way Lagerlöf employs the Nordic landscape and its mythology to demonstrate the complex and guilt-ridden interaction between family members and their environment when they are exposed to a threat originating in a repressed sense of disgrace and remorse.

Like Lagerlöf, several writers of today employ troll mythology to explore the kinship between trolls and humans but also to address issues of social alienation and exclusion as well as biological extinction. Stefan Spjut's two novels *Stallo* and *Stalpi* can be characterised as a documentation of trolls, in which the existence of trolls alongside with humans are proven believable. The story is set in the sparsely populated northern part of Sweden called Norrland, which represents the artic wilderness where unknown creatures and dying species on the verge of extinction may still dwell. Like Lindqvist's *Harbour*, the story opens like a crime novel about a missing child. In the prologue set in summer in the 1970s, a little boy disappears in the forest. In the main part of the novel, set in winter in 2004, another little boy is kidnapped. The latter abduction is connected to the appearance of a strange creature that the cryptozoologist Susso is asked to investigate by the kidnapped boy's grandmother. At the same time, the reader is introduced to an underground community of trolls and shapeshifters housed at a gated and remotely situated farm run by an odd family. Progressively, Spjut's story turns into an investigation of trolls as a still existing species and a study on what may happen when humans and trolls meet and breed.

The relationship and kinship between trolls and humans are multifaceted, at the same time as the depiction of the region of Norrland and the trolls as marginalised outcasts can be read as an ecocritical representation of marginalisation and extinction of lifeforms and species, according to Wijkmark and Adriana Margareta Dancus.[12] In Spjut's novels, trolls are depicted as different from humans, with qualities that set them apart and make them hard to control. They are shapeshifters and escape and hide in the shape of wild animals, and they are more adapted to harsh outdoor conditions than humans are. To communicate, they use telepathy and this skill makes them able to enter a human mind, to plant thoughts, erase memories and cause headache. These talents also make them able to develop close and uncanny relationship with certain persons in a way that changes the person's personality, that is, the distinction between the troll's and the human's minds dissolve, and thereby the difference between troll and human becomes arbitrary.

Apart from introducing zoological and ecological dimensions to the trolls, Spjut also presents the postcolonial history of their territory in northern Sweden. Several times in the novels, the protagonist Gudrun claims that the trolls disappeared when the region 'was electrified', that is, when industries and towns were built and lit up by electric light.[13] By that, trolls – and other wild species – were driven away to the unpopulated outskirts of the region, the shrinking areas of forests and fell in the artic part of Scandinavia that is still untouched by settlers. However, not only the Swedish colonisation and industrialisation endangered the habitat of trolls according to Spjut's story. The titles of the novels, *Stallo* and *Stalpi*, also allude to ancient Sámi myths of the Stallo people, who is believed to have inhabited the region before the Sámi people arrived. The actual historical existence of the Stallo people might be related to certain ancient remains called *Stallotomter* (Stallo settings) in the region. The Stallos are believed to have been driven away or extermi-nated during Sámi colonisation of the region and in Sámi mythology, Stallos are recognised as human-like giants, who are stupid and dangerous, and who prey on humans and abduct children. That is to say, the Stallos in Sámi myths are similar to trolls and giants in Swedish folklore. Spjut bases his fictional universe explicitly on these stories, at the same time as he refers to authentic archaeological findings in a way that turns his story into a semi-documentary. In that way, the distinction between myth and reality is blurred to highlight the possibility of a still existing ancient human-like species on the verge of extinction and how a humanoid species has been viewed from an anthropocentric perspective as a primitive and hostile lifeform. In that way, the multi-layered depiction of trolls and their interaction with the human protagonists is essential to the Gothic qualities of Spjut's story.

Humanised Trolls in Modern Society

Contrary to Stefan Spjut's troll fiction, John Ajvide Lindqvist's troll story *Border* is located close to the Swedish capital, Stockholm. It is about custom officer Tina, a modern professional woman that is exceptional good at detecting smugglers and their contraband. Although the American government has offered her a top position, she prefers to stay and work where she is born, the little port of Kapellskär by the Baltic Sea, about 90 kilometres north of Stockholm. Since childhood, she has developed a special relationship to the local landscape, the vast forest, which is confirmed when she once fails at work to find out what a suspected smuggler named Vores hides. She then escapes into the forest to handle her stressful experience. Deeply disturbed but also intrigued, Tina's meeting with Vore arouses repressed memories and feelings, and her relationship with Vore gradually reveals her origin, that is, she belongs to another ancient humanoid species described in myths and popular belief, that is, trolls.

In *Border*, the reader learns to know Tina from her internal viewpoint. Since childhood, she suffers from an experience of otherness, alienation and exclusion, mostly because of her physical appearance. A bit-by-lightening scar deforms her face making her unattractive and she also has a scar in her lower back above her tailbones. She is also set apart from other people by her exceptional sharp senses and by not being able to enjoy normal sex with her boyfriend because she finds it extremely painful. However, when she sets eyes on Vore, she recognises a masculine version of herself. His body odour also makes her feel safe. When he tells her that he finds her perfectly normal and confirms it when they have sex, she realises she is not human but something else. When she is introduced to Vore's hidden contraband, a *hiisit*, an unfertilised embryo that will soon die, she realises that he uses it as a changeling to kidnap a human baby. Tina's discovery makes her world crumble. When she confronts her father to find out the truth about her origin, he tells her that she was adopted after having been found in the forest and taken into custody because her mentally retarded parents were unable to care for her. Consequently, her parents were removed to a mental institution where they soon died. After having visited their grave and found out that they called her Reva, Tina reaches some kind of reconciliation and is able to respond to a message she receives from Vore at the end of the story.

Border is a story about identity and a person's painful discovery of not knowing who or what she is. Like in many of Lindqvist's stories, *Border* is about otherness, gender and sexual identity. Contrary to the vampire novel *Let the Right One In*, it is not about pre-pubertal romance but about a middle-aged woman's concept of love and gender because of her biological differences when she is judged by human norms. While Tina is unattractive because of her unfeminine looks, Vore is extremely masculine and looks '*too much* like a man' ('*för mycket* som en man');[14] his face is coarse and broad with protruding brows and a full beard, and his body is stout and muscular. Still, when Tina's male colleague searches him, he is not identified as a man, because he lacks male genitals. When he and Tina later have sex, Tina learns that she, not Vore, has a penis that is erect from her groins and that it is he, and not she, that is able to become pregnant and bear a child. Thereby, the couple Tina and Vores reverses the sexual biology of humans, at the same time as they in daily life act according to the prevailing gender roles in human society; Tina behaves according to female norms, while Vore is by his appearance and behaviour identified as a man.

To Tina, the experience of otherness is very much a mental and social issue. Since childhood, she has suffered from her unfeminine features, which she considers as an abnormal deformity and a personal drawback, especially in her relationships with men. The scar on her low back and the unbearable pain she felt when she once had intercourse with her partner trouble her. Contrariwise, she is brought up as a human girl and therefore she has integrated human norms of social and biological qualities. Her sharp senses, especially hearing and sense of smell, are of advantage to her as a custom officer and in her interaction with humans as she is easily able to detect and identify human emotions. Her close connection to nature, plants and animals, she finds normal as she was brought up at a farm in the forest. Her fondness for uncooked raw food, she does not pay much attention to until Vore offers her worms to eat and she realises that unlike humans, she prefers this kind of diet. When she discovers that her physical particularities – her scars and genitals – cannot be explained as human deformities but is a result of her true troll nature, she breaks down. She throws out her partner, takes sick leave and isolates herself at home. To what extent she actually accepts her true nature and new identity is left unanswered. At the end of the story, Tina goes back to work and when Vore returns, she knows that he bears their child. When she goes to meet him, the reader does not know if it is to do her job and catch him or if she intends to join him and form a troll family with him and their expected child.

Before it is spelt out in *Border*, Tina and Vore are by the Swedish reader identified as trolls, at the same time as they modify what is known about trolls and changelings from myths and folktales. Like trolls, they are described as ugly according to human norms and their scars in their lower back indicate that they were born with a tail that has been removed by surgery. They are described as nature lovers that prefer spending time in the forest to leading an indoor life in front of the screen. However, neither Tina nor Vore appears to be typical changelings. Tina's parents have not traded her for her foster parents' human baby. Her foster parents have adopted her because her biological parents were not believed to provide for her and she has developed a close and loving relationship with her foster father. Vore's childhood is not revealed but he seems to have been brought up to both embrace his troll nature and navigate as a troll in a human society. Unlike trolls in folktales and myths, Tina and Vore behave like most people; they speak human language and they know how to socialise with human people.

Lindqvist's novella also differs from most stories about trolls and changelings in choice of viewpoint. In Swedish folklore and literature, including Lagerlöf's and Spjut's troll fiction, the troll is depicted from an external androcentric perspective as an alien creature that represents untamed nature and poses a threat to humans and human civilisation. *Border*, however, is narrated from the troll's – Tina's – internal point of view, and it is even partly told by Tina when sections of her diary are inserted in the story. Thereby, it is not the troll but the human beings that are viewed from an external perspective. In particular, Tina's human partner Roland is externalised and unfamiliarised when Tina observes him in front of the TV-set and thinks he looks like a monster in the light from the screen. Accordingly, there is at first no clear and established distinction between trolls and humans in *Border*; it is from a humanised troll's perspective the differences and the essence of human nature are explored, and it is the troll, not the humans, that deserves the reader's sympathy. From Tina's viewpoint, the reader engages in her search for identity. At first, she looks upon her physical ugliness and defects as caused by accident or as congenital deformity. After she has met Vore, she gradually realises that her mentally and physically nature as a troll differs from human nature and the prevailing human heterosexual norms. By then, she is split between her innate troll nature and the human moral and social norms she has internalised when she was brought up in a human community. In Lindqvist novella, her identity crisis is also linked to certain environmental and postcolonial issues. As Wijkmark points out, the trolls in Lindqvist's story represent the good ecocritical ideology. They live in harmony with nature while humans exploit it.[15] In particular, Vore is a spokesperson for this ideological message. He tells Tina that human expansion is the reason why there are so few trolls left on earth and that those few still living have been forced to adapt to human norms. Therefore, they have lost their identity as trolls. It is because of this that he operates as part of an underground troll movement and as a resistance fighter by bereaving human parents of their children. When his assignment is revealed to Tina, she is even more torn between her troll nature and her human morals and social duties.

If Tina's identity crisis is the central theme of Lindqvist's novella, the underlying postcolonial message is more prominent in Ali Abbasi's film *Border* (2018) based on Lindqvist story. In it, Tina (Eva Melander) and Vore (Eero Minonoff) are given strongly Neanderthal appearances that immediately sets them apart as belonging to another human race or humanoid species. At the same time, they look so much alike as if they were family, almost as if they

were siblings. When they are seen together in the forest, their otherness is
even more accentuated. From the opening of the film, Tina is depicted as
a nature lover with a close relationship with wild animals but when Vore
joins her in the forest, they both turn into nature beings belonging to another
primitive species different from modern human beings. Vore introduces her
to eat living insects and to set aside what she has been taught about proper
food during her upbringing in human society. Together with Vore, she also
learns to communicate with new facial expressions and guttural sounds that
seem to come natural to her. Her sense of smell and how she relies on it is
also accentuated in Abbasi's adaptation by close-up pictures of her vibrating
nostrils. In that way, Tina and Vore's kinship is proven to the audience, at the
same time as their differences from other humans is stressed, especially when
they have intercourse and Tina, not Vore, is showed with an erect penis.
Contrary to Lindqvist's novella, the sex scene in Abbasi's film takes place
in wild nature, on the moss-covered ground in the forest, which even more
highlights Tina and Vore as being closer to nature than modern humans are.

In an interview, director Abbasi claims that Tina's experience of being
an outsider can be compared with living in Sweden as an ethnic minority.[16]
By that, he points at the underlying political and postcolonial aspects of the
film. In the film, the setting highlights Tina as a migrant between different
spheres in current Sweden, most distinctly the official modern society and the
remaining wilderness beyond human settlements. In the first sphere, she acts
in uniform and represents Swedish law enforcement as a proficient custom
officer and crime investigator in modern urban indoor environments, such
as the arrival hall for passengers at the harbour, at the police station, in the
police car and while she is searching some suspected paedophiles' apartment
in the city. In the second private sphere, she seems perfectly confident when
she is interacting with wild animals and is strolling along barefoot in the
forest or swimming naked in a forest lake. Between these two spheres, she is
also seen engaged in private relationships with other people. Although she
has a close bond with her old disabled foster father, she looks awkward and
intimidated together with other persons. For example, she appears distant
and unable to socialise with her partner Roland, in particular in front of the
TV screen and at the dinner table. While she rejects him when he approaches
her in bed, she welcomes the visit of a wild fox outside the bedroom window.
At the same time as her dysfunctional relationship with Roland is repeatedly
confirmed, her difference and outsider status are stated.

Although Tina's affinity with Vore is progressively demonstrated on the
screen, they handle their experience of otherness and marginalisation in
different ways. While Vore denies being human and despises human society,
Tina embraces human morals and the significance of empathy and care. In

the film, he is not only kidnapping human babies; he is also working for a global organisation of infant trafficking. In that way, he seeks retribution; his replacement of human infants with dying troll embryo is organised by the trolls to get their revenge on human for the trolls that humans tortured in the 1970s. According to Tina, the human mistreatment of trolls in the past does not justify such vengeful acts and therefore she tries to stop Vore. The conflict is strengthened as Tina as a custom officer is working in the police team that tries to stop a paedophilia organisation and their trafficking of infants. Although she reveals Vore's crime to her team in order to stop him, he escapes the police by jumping into the sea from a ferry. He also appears to have survived as the film ends when Tina receives a parcel with a troll infant together with a postcard from Finland. Although the audience does not know how Tina will deal with the child and her new situation, the film addresses, as Rebecca Pulsifer claims, different forms of care.[17] Compared to Lindqvist's novella, Abassi's film accentuates the importance of care for other social groups, species and lifeforms. Nevertheless, and just as Lindqvist's story, Abbasi's film explores what it is being human, if it is based on appearance or actions, a product of nature or culture. Moreover, significant to the exploration of this theme is the Nordic concept of trolls, the ideas of these mythical creatures' relationship to wild nature and human civilisation.

Swedish Wilderness Gothic

Swedish Gothic could be called *Wilderness Gothic*. The Nordic landscape is a space of fear, both a haunted and a haunting space that is inhabited with devious mythical creatures known from myths and popular belief. It is a malevolent and dangerous space located beyond places of civilisation and urban modernity. In Nordic folktales and popular imagination, the forest is associated with danger, supernatural phenomenon and pagan powers of nature. However, in Swedish Gothic, also other places of wilderness represent hostile powers of untamed nature. Recent stories are often set in the sparsely populated region of northern Sweden, in the vast artic areas of Nordic fells and ancient forests. Spjut's novels *Stallo* and *Stalpi* are illustrative examples of the desolate and sparsely populated region of Norrland as a remaining habitat of ancient lifeforms and nowadays repressed creatures of myths, such as trolls. Lagerlöf's *Lord Arne's Silver* and Lindqvist's *Harbour* explore the labyrinthine waterscape of the archipelago as a space ruled by mysterious powers. In Lagerlöf's story about crime and punishment, the frozen waterscape outside Marstrand is an aggressive protagonist that triggers violence and crime by raising supernatural beings, such as werewolves and vengeance-seeking revenants. In Lindqvist's novel, the scenery and powers of nature act in another overpowering way by invading and controlling the minds of the protagonist. Contrary to in *Lord Arne's Silver* and most nineteenth-century Gothic, good does not triumph over evil and human conditions of normality is not re-established. Instead, Lindqvist's story ends in a state of uncertainty and ambiguity.

That is to say, the Nordic wilderness has gone wilder and more uncontrollable in the last decades. The androcentric position and perspective are progressively contested and the encounter between the urban protagonist and untamed nature is predestined to end in chaos and loss of human identity. The duality between the protagonist and the local environment and its indigenous population is central to the Gothic atmosphere. While the visiting protagonists are defined by their mobility and lack of permanent relationship with the local environment, the native inhabitants are one with their territory and landscape. Although Anders in Lindqvist's *Harbour* is born and bred on the island of Domarö, his move to the capital has turned him into a typical protagonist of today's Swedish Gothic. Outside the city, he is a misplaced tourist; to him the archipelago has transformed into a place of loss and absence, a haunted space that affects and transforms his perception. Progressively, he finds himself possessed in a way that enhances his – and the reader's – awareness of the coastal landscape's impenetrable complexity. His experiences are what the ecological philosopher Timothy Morton calls *interconnectedness*, an idea of embodied perception and mutual connection with everything he encounters in the archipelago.[18] The withholding of narrative closure in current Gothic stories such as *Harbour* intensified the depiction of the non-urban landscape as a transformative space where uncanny experiences occur. It becomes a wild space that triumphs over man-made structures and humanised space as place. It becomes a mythical space where the chronological time does not exist and where the protagonist enters a realm of eternal present or timelessness.

The mythical dimensions of the Nordic setting are even more prominent in troll fiction. It is an example of EcoGothic that seeks to challenge the anthropocentric gaze on nature and thereby indorses the intrinsic interconnectedness with a variety of human and non-human lifeforms.[19] Troll fiction, such as Spjut's *Stallo* and Lindqvist's *Border*, go beyond the conventional Gothic conception of nature and its creatures as threatening to depict them as acting, alien others with their own logic and psychological complexity. As an alien and hostile lifeform, the trolls pose both a threat and a mystery. Although the plot revolves around the suspenseful and dramatic confrontations between trolls and humans, the core of the mystery in these stories is the kinship between the two species and the progressively blurred distinction between the trolls and humans. Thereby, it also clearly demonstrates what Dancus finds characteristic of current troll fiction, the environmental friction between humans and trolls and that the two species are equally endangered due to their vulnerability and capacity to harm each other.[20]

In Lindqvist's *Border* and Abassis film based on the story, the distinction between troll and human is more dubious than in most Gothic troll fiction. By the use of the troll as the protagonist and by the use of internal focalisation, the battle between troll and human is not located in an exterior landscape of wilderness, but in an inner landscape of mental struggle and chaos. The socialised humanised troll's search for identity is not only demonstrating what it means being human but in addition all lifeforms and species interconnectedness with nature, that is, both nature as an outer environment and as inborn biological and mental qualities. However, the portrayal of the troll's conflict does not result in a reduction to savagery, rather in a reduction of human dominance and humanity as an exclusive human quality.

Chapter 2

THE GENDER-CODED LANDSCAPE AND TRANSGRESSIVE FEMALE MONSTERS

Since the second half of the nineteenth century, it is possible to make a distinction between two gendered tendencies in Swedish Gothic that are both identified with the gender of the writer and the gender of the fictional protagonist. Furthermore, it is possible to distinguish between what Anne Williams calls a Male formula and a Female formula in terms of plot, narrative technique, gendered point of view and use of supernatural elements.[1] However, the formula is not the same as in Anglo-American Gothic. Although some Swedish women writers portray imprisoned and victimised heroines, they are not as confined and perpetuated by male tyrants as Kate Ferguson Ellis claims them to be in 'feminine Gothic' originated from Ann Radcliffe's stories.[2] Nor does the Swedish version of Male Gothic expose a plot of masculine transgression of social norms and taboos. Thereby, it does not fulfil that kind of Male formula that Diana Wallace, Andrew Smith and others have identified as Anglo-American Male Gothic from Matthew Lewis onwards.[3]

Both the Male and Female formulas of Swedish Gothic revolve around the devious Nordic wilderness. Many stories by Swedish male writers and film directors are set in a hostile landscape and revolve around the male protagonist's meeting with an alluring female being, sometimes a creature from Swedish folklore. At the same time as she represents untamed nature, she also demonstrates that forces of nature are dependent on female agency. In that way, the Swedish version of Male Gothic confirms a recurrent motif in today's EcoGothic that Elisabeth Parker calls 'Monstrous Mother Natures' or 'the She-Devil in the Wilderness'.[4] In the female version of Swedish Gothic, women writers explore gendered concept of the Nordic scenery and its mythological creatures. Since the late nineteenth century, they have employed the formula of Anglo-American Female Gothic to communicate gendered issues, and since the millennium, a female subgenre of Gothic stories has emerged, in which the female protagonist is both persecutor and prey. Instead of being a victimised heroine, the female character develops supernatural powers or exceptional knowledge of magic. In addition, in today's many stories targeting young female adults, the protagonist is often a witch or a collective of witches, who is assigned to participate in an ongoing struggle between good and evil forces in nature in order to save the world.

This chapter gives a survey of the two gendered tendencies in Swedish Gothic from the late nineteenth century with emphasis on the Swedish setting and the employment of local folk beliefs. First, it demonstrates the emergence of a male tradition from Viktor Rydberg's novel *Singoalla* (*Singoalla*, 1857) to today's Gothic stories and horror films about female nature beings operating in a hostile Swedish landscape by male writers and directors, such as Tommy Wiklund and Sony Laguna's film *Wither* (*Vittra*, 2012) and Anders Fager's story 'The Furies from Borås' ('Furierna från Borås', 2011). Second, it explores women writers' use of Gothic elements from Selma Lagerlöf's novels *Gösta Berling's Saga* (*Gösta Berlings saga*, 1891) and *A Manor House Tale* (*En herrgårdsägen*, 1899) until current young-adult fiction. The focus will be on women writers' employment of a regional setting and local folklore or history to address gendered issues in stories such as Majgull Axelson's novel *April Witch* (*Aprilhäxan*, 1997) and Madeleine Bäck's crossover trilogy – *The Water Draws* (*Vattnet drar*, 2015), *The Soil Arouses* (*Jorden vaknar*, 2017) and *The Mountain Sacrifices* (*Berget offrar*, 2018).

An Early Female Vampire

An early example of a victimised male protagonist and feminised powers of nature is Viktor Rydberg's most popular novel *Singoalla*. Rydberg rewrote the novel three times throughout his life. The first version of 1857 is the most plot-driven story with many horror effects and the most heart-breaking ending. In the final version of 1894, the religious theme and the use of poetic symbols are extended and the novel concludes with the protagonist, Erland Måneskiöld, becoming a hermit monk. Whichever version of the novel, it is about two star-crossed lovers, a Swedish crusader, Erland, and a foreign pagan girl, Singoalla, who belongs to the nomadic Romani people. The first part of the novel describes the young couple's passionate meetings at night in the woods in order to avoid their reluctant families' notice and it ends when Erland is returned to his father's castle, where his family's priest tries to erase his memories of Singoalla. The second part takes place many years later, when Singoalla sends her and Erlands son, Sorgebarn, to Erland's castle in order to enable their reunion. Sorgebarn's arrival and stay at the castle stirs Erland's repressed memories and he is increasingly plagued by nightmarish visions of Singoalla until he in a fit of rage kills Sorgebarn. Plagued by regret, the anguished Erland raves around in the forest, at the same time as the plague hits his people. In the first version of the novel, Erland is reunited with Singoalla in the desolate Nordic wilderness before he dies with his head in her lap. In later versions of the novel, Erland and Singoalla part after the death of Sorgebarn, and Erland spends the rest of his life making atonements as a hermit monk by a creek in the forest.

Erland and Singoalla's love story is described in a Gothic mode, and in 1923, the Swedish scholar Viktor Svanberg compared it to Gautier's *The Dead Woman in Love* (*La morte amoreuse*, 1836).[5] Like Gautier's vampire story, it describes a young man torn between his Christian duties and his forbidden desire for an attractive woman, who haunts him in hallucinatory visions at night. As I have argued elsewhere, the use of blood, moon and night increases the Gothic mode of Rydberg's story.[6] Right from the beginning, Erland and Singoalla's relationship is tainted by blood and violence. They meet in the forest when one of Erland's hunting dogs approaches to attack Singoalla and she turns towards Erland with the dog's blood dripping from her knife. Her unexpected and unfeminine behaviour, in combination with her exotic beauty, charms the young man. Possessed by love, Erland sneaks out at night to meet his beloved by a creek in the forest, where they one moonlit night are secretly united by blood oath, according to the animist rituals used by Singoalla's people. Although Erland is returned to his Christian home, wedded to his intended Christian bride and prepared for his assignment as a crusader by his priest, his conjugal union with Singoalla, sanctioned by her moon god, cannot be brought to nothing, not even by the priest's fierce exorcism. When Erland and Singoalla's son Sorgebarn arrives to the castle to reunite his parents, he uses seeds picked in full moonlight to put Erland into a hypnotic somnambulistic state with the intention to bring him to Singoalla's cave. With these seeds, Erland's repressed memories re-emerge and he becomes his young self, madly in love with Singoalla. Soon, Erland cannot keep apart his two personalities, Singoalla's lover and the married Christian crusader. During the day at home in his castle, he is increasingly haunted by the fragmented visions of Singoalla as an evil nocturnal creature. When he once catches sight of her in daylight, he even calls her a vampire and witch. Not until he kills Sorgebarn one night, and thereby the blood-related link between him and Singoalla is cut off, he is able to accept and unite his past and present history and personality.

Singoalla is one of those characters Glennis Byron calls 'monstrous metaphoric female figures' of the late nineteenth-century Gothic.[7] At the same time as she is depicted as a seductive female vampire, she shares features with female beings in Swedish folklore, such as *Älvdrottningen* (the Fairy Queen) and *Skogsrået* (the Mistress of the Forest). Like these two creatures, Singoalla is extremely attractive and a nature being that primarily operates in twilight. Erland meets her in moonlight at night in the forest, either by a creek or in a cave, and often he cannot separate her shape from the background. Like *Älvdrottningen* in medieval Nordic ballads, she seduces a young Christian knight and their meeting leads to his destruction; although *Älvdrottningen's* male victim in the ballads often is returned to his castle, it is in a state of mental disorder or insanity, from which he never recovers. Erland's fate also recalls popular stories about human men, who are seduced by *Skogsrået*; their souls will always remain with her, and if they betray her or are unfaithful to her, they will be punished by misfortunes and accidents.

However, Erland is not as good and innocent as most male victims in Nordic myths are. He is like many male protagonists in Romantic Gothic both victim and villain, as Fred Botting points out.[8] He is by birth destined to be enticed to Singoalla and the pagan animism she and her people represent. His family is by their family name Måneskiöld, meaning *Moon shield*, linked to the moon and the powers of nature. Erland's father also fears for the family's barbaric past and that Erland takes after one of his ancestors, known for his wild temper and for worshipping the old Nordic gods. In that way, Erland is not only prone to be attracted to the passionate Singoalla and her worship of nature but also to recognise and activate his and his family's pagan past.

Gendered Nature in Recent Male Gothic

A male protagonist's fatal encounter with creatures of nature, often personified by an attractive or beloved woman, is a recurrent theme in today's Swedish Gothic. In many stories by male writers and directors, untamed nature assumes female qualities and a construction of feminine identity as monstrous or as an expression of cultural anxiety. Several novels and films from the late twentieth century onwards depict a group of people's journey from the city and their weird experiences in a remote area beyond modern civilisation. In several cases, the stories revolve around the male protagonist's experience of alienation and often the horrors are associated with creatures from Nordic myths and folktales. In Tommy Wiklund and Sony Laguna's film *Wither*, the young city-dwellers' weekend trip to an abandoned cottage in the forest initiates a life-and-death struggle. The danger emanates from a female creature in the cellar that comes to life and immediately influences one of the girls and makes her change into an attacking monster. To the partying youths, the wither's victims transform into hybrids of vampire and zombie, whose bite and blood contaminate their preys and turn them into the same kind of non-human monster. At the end of the film, the last survivor, the male protagonist, witnesses his girlfriend's transformation into a menacing wither.

Wither can be categorised as a transnational horror film with a regional twist. Many Swedish and international critics recognised it as a Swedish version of Sam Raimi's *The Evil Dead* (1981).[9] In addition, there are obvious references to other iconic films, such as Stanley Kubrick's *The Shining*. It could also be seen as a Swedish version of what is called American *cabin horror*, where the isolated cabin in the forest gives the illusion of refuge against the lurking monster in the woods.[10] However – and contrary to many Anglo-American horror films – the cottage in *Wither* is from the beginning the site of monstrous wilderness. The film also demonstrates a reverse gender order, where the monster is not male but female and she clearly prefers female targets, both in the present time of narration and in the previous story told in flashbacks. In the film, the pursued *final girl* is replaced by a virtuous young man, a *final boy*, who is able to maintain his human nature and survive and fight his contaminated pals. However, for a start everything indicates that the film will end with the final girl as the survivor. When the only human survivors in the cottage are the young heroic couple, Ida (Lisa Henni) and Albin (Patrik Almkvist), who host the weekend party and endanger their own lives in order to help and save their guests, he is repeatedly hurt and twice it looks as if he is lost. However, because of Ida's affection for her brother, who returns and infects her, she starts to transform in front of Albin's eyes. Because she refrains from attacking him in those moments she recognises her lover, he is eventually able to kill her off. Therefore, and unlike most endangered men in Nordic folktales about female creatures of nature, the male protagonist in *Wither* does not only escape, but he also defeats the wither. Thus, he fulfils the role of a teenage hero in popular horror films targeting young adults. In the very end, when the wither (Jessica Blomkvist) ascends from the cellar, Albin crushes her by flinging a refrigerator towards her. That is, the young male hero eliminates the female creature of Nordic myths by using the most modern piece of equipment in the cottage, an appliance for high-tech food preservation. His gender-transgressive behaviour is even more stressed when he as the final boy survives the monster not by means of a male-coded weapon but by using a modern appliance from the once female domain of the cottage, the kitchen and its storeroom.

The reversed and masculinised gender formula in *Wither* is also noticeable in other ways. Although the Swedish title of the film, *Vittra*, refers to a nature spirit and a mythological creature from the northern half of Sweden, the monster is a mixture of zombie and vampire that has few features in common with the wither in Swedish folklore. According to popular belief, withers are invisible creatures keeping cattle and living underground, or in abandoned human lodges; they dwell in a parallel universe to that of human farmers. Normally, they do not meddle in human affairs but they might act menacing when they are not respected or become enraged, for example, if humans interfere in their territory, build their homes on top of their world or block their passages. If provoked, they might arrange accidents that will harm or kill their human intruders. In the film *Wither*, the visitors intrude when they break into the locked cottage by sending one of the girls in, who on her own behalf visits the cellar, the habitat of a solitary female wither. However, the lurking wither in Wiklund and Laguna's film does not avenge the intrusion by causing accidents, but by turning the first trespasser into a contagious and violent female killer, whose attacks transform her peers into zombie vampires. Still, the old wither's pagan nature as an evil creature of untamed nature is confirmed when she finally ascends from the cellar, which happens when Alvin repeatedly and in shock three times has cried out *Fan*, a Swedish swearword meaning *The Devil* or *Satan*. When he the third time repeats *Fan* twice, she finally appears from her domains as conjured up by his invocation.

Thus, the gendered female threat is repeatedly stated in *Wither*. In the main plot, the wither's first and only victim is a girl, and it is this infected girl who triggers the catastrophe. When the wither eventually ascends from the cellar to inspect her ruined territory, her ancient nature is emphasised. In front of the camera, she appears withered and timeworn, a menacing but fragile old woman. Her vulnerability is accentuated when she in front of a window turns her back to Albin as if to encourage him to attack her and she is easily killed by the weight of the refrigerator. In that way, the young, fit male Albin kills his girlfriend and the wither in a similar way, by smashing them by throwing a heavy piece of furniture at them, a bookcase and a refrigerator, respectively.

However, not all male protagonists are as lucky as Albin in Wiklund and Laguna's film *Wither*. One of the most violent examples of gendered wilderness and female ferocity is the opening story in Anders Fager's *Collected Swedish Cults* (*Samlade svenska kulter*, 2011), a collection of horror stories that are related to each other in an uncanny way.[11] The opening story 'The Furies from Borås' is an illustrative example of what P.H. Lovecraft calls *cosmic fear* stemming from a dread of unknown alien forces beyond human experience and exceeding the laws of nature.[12] It describes some young girls on their way for a party night in the woods outside the textile-manufacturing town Borås in western Sweden. For a start, they behave as most young partygoers equipped with makeup and party drugs and they are full of expectations to find the perfect boy. However, soon their preparations appear to be part of a collective well-planed scheme of choosing and abducting an easily seduced male for ritual purposes, that is, to bring him into the woods and offer him to an old gluttonous creature that hides in the marchlands. The increasingly fierce sexual performance of the girls, or *furies from Borås*, and the increasingly precarious situation of their victim, is brutally described. So are also the girls' actions as part of archaic cults and occult rituals of human sacrifice that the girls and their foremothers have been preordained to perform for generations. At the same time as the girls are described as victimised female sadists, their ritual violence appears to be part of keeping the forces of untamed nature under control. The rituals they perform are intended both to satisfy the creature's voyeuristic desires and to feed its appetite for human flesh. To do that require female desire and carnal agency, but if the girls fail, they risk being taken by the creature themselves and thereby to be incorporated in its herd of *young ones*. In that way, Fager's story is an illustrative example of today's Swedish Male Gothic where young women figure the fatal and sexual intensity of nature, or the sexual part of nature as dependent on female desire.

Female Creatures of Untamed Nature by Women Writers

Since the late nineteenth century, women writers have explored Nordic wilderness in connection to gender issues and female identity. One of the most famous and influential examples from the *fin de siècle* is Selma Lagerlöf. As demonstrated in the previous chapter, untamed nature plays a vital part as a carrier of repressed emotions and as a vehicle to re-establish order and justice in for example *Lord Arne's Silver*. In some of the novels, untamed nature is represented by a female creature of nature. One of her most uncanny images of wilderness and decay is *Fru Sorg* (Mrs Sorrow) in *A Manor House Tale*. The story revolves around two young protagonists, Gunnar and Ingrid, who eventually save each other from mental disorder and death. Crucial for their salvation is Ingrid's confrontation with *Fru Sorg*, an ill-omened figure that is dressed up in a coat of black bats that flutter and take off when she opens her covering. Her recurrent visits to Gunnar's inherited estate illustrate the accelerating decay of the manor and the decline of its source of income, the ironworks. At the same time as her frightening appearances sums up the sorrows and shame in connection with the manor and its family, it demonstrates the rule of nature and the fragility of human civilisation. If not looked after, the estate will be taken over by wilderness, and thereby, the family is doomed to decline and ruin. It is not until Ingrid recognises the power of *Fru Sorg* and is prepared to fight her that she is able to rescue Gunnar from insanity and his family and home from extinction.

Fru Sorg is more of a threatening image than an active force in *A Manor House Tale* while Lagerlöf's novel *Gösta Berling's Saga* is populated with several aggressive and acting creatures of nature. The episodic novel revolves around the charming Don Juan-character Gösta Berling, a defrocked minister who is rescued from death by *Majorskan*, the powerful mistress of the ironwork estate Ekeby. Together, with eleven other failed men, he becomes one of the *chavaliers* or pensioners at Ekeby. One Christmas night, Gösta and the pensioners are duped to lead an uprising against their benefactor in order to seize control of Ekeby. During the year of their reign, various powers of nature – or the landscape as such – rise against their reckless lifestyle by causing floods, drought and bad harvests. The population of the area is also afflicted by various mythological creatures of nature, such as the killer bear from the mountain Gurlitta klätt, and various uncanny female beings, such as *Skogsfrun* (the Mistress of the Forests) and *Dovres häxa* (the Witch from Dovre Mountain). When *Skogsfrun* first approaches one of the *chavaliers*, the wannabe inventor Kevenhüller, she endows him with originality and creativity on one condition; his inventions are not to be multiplied. When he during the year of the *chavaliers'* reign comes up with his masterpiece, a wheel of fire, he starts to dream about mass production for the benefit of poor people. His defiance is just about to end in destruction when *Skogsfrun* arrives and reclaims her gift, at the same time as she stops the estate of Ekeby from burning down.

However, the most terrible creature of untamed nature is not *Skogsfrun* but *Dovres häxa*. The witch's harassment and cruelty do not hit one of the *chavaliers* but the malevolent Lady Märta Donna, who tyrannises all women in her household, in particular her daughter-in-law, the virtuous Elisabeth. As a punishment for her brutality, the witch sends Märta Donna a flight of aggressive blackbirds that are ready to attack her whenever she shows up outside her mansion. Thereby, she is for the rest of her life imprisoned in her home, at the same time as everybody is reminded of her misconducts. The attacking blackbirds are both a punishment and a representation of her vicious mind and previous crimes. In *Gösta Berling's Saga*, both *Skogsfrun* and *Dovres häxa* are powerful examples of female agency, at the same time as they act to punish transgressors, no matter male or female, in order to save a worthy woman or her territory, such as Majorskan and her Ekeby.

Selma Lagerlöf's way of employing menacing female creatures of nature to highlight and deal with ethical and gendered issues has inspired later novelists. The portrayal of a woman gifted with exceptional mental resources and a strong bond to nature, in combination with a moral mission reoccurs in Majgull Axelsson's novel *April Witch*. The protagonist Desirée is assigned to what Juliann E. Fleenor calls a female religious quest that proves to be for a deceitful ideal defined by a patriarchal society.[13] Desirée is motherless and physically disabled and she sees herself as absolutely abandoned by her family, society and God. Because of that, she illustrates that Fleenor sees as fundamental to Female Gothic, an internalised ambivalence to the female, both the good and evil aspect of it.[14]

Axelsson's Desirée is abandoned at birth because of her disabilities – cerebral palsy, epilepsy and physical deformation – and all her life she has been restrained to institutions and nursing homes. Now a middle-aged paralysed woman, she tracks her biological mother's three foster daughters, her foster sisters, with the aim of obtaining redress. In order to accomplish her operation, she develops supernatural powers of omniscience to investigate the life of her mother, the *betrayer*, and her sisters, the *thieves*, who stole her childhood and the life that should belong to her. In her quest for truth and justification, the dying Desirée, sees herself as an *April Witch* that moves around mentally by taking residence in living animals, sometimes also in healthy humans in order to track and control her sisters.

Desirée is right from the beginning a transgressive Gothic character with exceptional supernatural talents; she is able to occupy the bodies and minds of other living beings, and in that way, she is able to enslave them according to her scheme. She is also a double, an extremely confined and vulnerable woman in a dying body but with a powerful mind and paranormal skills. The aim of her actions is to evoke fear and harm, at the same time as her pursuit unveils conditions that facilitate her own redemption. However, the power balance between Desirée and her sisters shifts, thereby also altering the conventional relationship between persecutor and victim. In the beginning, she is in control and superior to her ignorant victims but because every visionary journey costs her one of her remaining physical abilities, her mission is fatal and will end with her death. Thus, the question that drives the plot is: Will she be able to conclude her mission before she dies, or will it all end in death and destruction both for her and her victims?

The ambivalent character of Desirée and her undertaking is stressed by her name *April Witch*. While Selma Lagerlöf's *Dovres häxa* (the Witch of Dovre Mountain) in *Gösta Berling's Saga* is connected to the wild powers of a certain Nordic landscape and a specific mountain, Axelson's *April Witch* is allied to a season and month. In Scandinavia, the month of April marks the transition from winter to spring and it is known to be a month of changeable weather and unreliable conditions. The expression *aprilväder* in Swedish (weather of April) means quickly changing weather, from cold and squalls of snow to sunshine and warmth within less than an hour. Thus, the label *April Witch* stresses Desirée's double and unreliable nature.

The names of Lagerlöf's and Axelson's witches also indicate that they are no traditional witches associated with brews, evil spells and devil-worship, that is, those features that marked a woman accused of witchcraft during the witch trials in history. Instead, they are by their names linked to nature and, thereby, like many creatures of nature in Swedish literature; they operate as vehicles of justice. In both novels, their targets are women who have wronged other women, and their missions are to restore order in society. However, there is a significant difference between Lagerlöf's and Axelson's witches.

Contrary to Lagerlöf's witch, the reader learns to know Axelson's Desirée from internal focalisation; she is the protagonist of the novel and she controls both the narration and the plot. She introduces herself as an *April Witch* and by the Italian concept of *benandanti*, so-called *good walker*, and she informs the reader about the *benandanti* community. Despite being invalid, Desirée believes herself to be born with a caul on her head and with innate powers of leaving her disabled body for visionary journeys. As a member of the *benandanti* community and its struggle against malevolent witches (*maladanti*), her mission is to overthrow the power of abusive women in her life, that is, her biological mother's three foster daughters. However, when she has learnt to know her sisters and been informed about their backgrounds, failures and present life, she changes her mind and instead of ruining their lives, she reunites them and possibly improves their chances for a better future together.

Desirée's idea of being a *benandanti* is imbued with Swedish folklore. Her information about the *benandanti* community and its celebration of four seasonal holidays prompts Swedish popular belief about ancient pagan holidays associated with the powers of nature, pre-Christian deities and witchcraft. Her visionary excursions also remind the reader of Nordic ideas of *byta hamn*, that is to inhabit or take possession of the body and mind of another being. In the beginning, she travels in the shape of a black crow bird, a recurring bird in Swedish mythology that is connected to the most powerful ancient pagan god Oden. Later on, she inhabits other birds, such as seagulls, before she enters and takes possession of a number of human bodies and minds, in a way that both benefits her aims and strengthens her bond to supernatural shapeshifting creatures in Nordic mythology.

Desirée's supernatural powers of omniscience serve to highlight different aspects of the Swedish society. Thus, Axelson's novel is an illustrative example of a combination of supernatural terror and social realism. Although Desirée is the protagonist, the bulk of the novel revolves around her three sisters and their upbringing as foster children from the 1950s onwards. One of them, Margareta, was abandoned at birth and found in a laundry, while the other two girls, Christina and Birgitta, were partially raised by abusive mothers. Whereas Margareta and Christina have managed to adapt to the demands of society and a career as a physicist and a physician respectively, Birgitta lives at the margins of society as an alcoholic. In that way, the three cases demonstrate different aspects of Swedish childcare and its consequences related to individual circumstances. The story exposes deficiencies in the welfare system both when it comes to disabled children, such as Desirée, and children neglected by their parents, such as Christina and Birgitta. In that way, the women and their backgrounds demonstrate different aspects of social rejection and that some citizens are not benefitting from the welfare system, in particular not certain groups of women and children. When Desirée starts to interfere in her sisters' lives in order to manipulate them in certain directions, it first appears to be part of her revenge; her actions pose immediate danger to the three intended victims. However, instead of sending her sisters into a Gothic underworld of nightmare, Desirée progressively invites them on individual quests that lead to restoration and reconciliation. The new afflictions they have to face make them re-evaluate both their present way of living and their more or less repressed past, at the same time as they reconcile as sisters with a shared history. In that way, the true victim turns out to be Desirée. Although she acts as an *April Witch* and a capable monster, she turns out to be the ultimate victimised female heroine. She is imprisoned in two ways, in an institution and in a disabled and diseased body, and every outbreak shortens her life. Each visionary journey results in loss of control, to be exact, those few muscles in her mouth that she is still able to control and uses to communicate. Explicitly, because of her visionary journeys, she is right from the beginning destined to loss and extinction.

Crossover Witchcraft at the Millennium

Like in Majgull Axelson's *April Witch*, Madeleine Bäck's crossover trilogy – *The Water Draws*, *The Soil Arouses* and *The Mountain Sacrifices* – explores various ideas of good and evil witchcraft. In addition, Bäck's trilogy firmly promotes local Swedish lore about ironworks. The trilogy is set in mining district of Gästrikland in Sweden, and the young protagonists find themselves subject to old forces of nature and myths connected to the local pit, as well as to the region's disturbing past of blood-spattered battles and large-scale witch trials. At the same time as mythological manifestations of nature attack them, they are mentally taken over by devious forces, inner voices and tantalising desires. The story opens when some young criminals steal a medieval Madonna statue from the local church and one of them, Viktor, finds a walled-in stone under the alter. At the same time as he explores the magic powers of the stone, a young woman, Beata, finds her girlfriend being seduced by a disturbing boyfriend, while a young man, Krister, is plagued by a recurrent nightmare that drains him of energy.

If Axelson refers to the Italian concepts *benandanti* and *malandanti*, Bäck uses Swedish names, *väktare* (watchers) and *vandrare* (walkers). Like Axelson's *April Witch*, Bäck's watchers are undertaking visionary journeys by entering another being's mind and body to gain information or to possess their preys. Thereby, Bäck's watchers clearly demonstrate the Nordic concept *byta hamn*, that is, to change harbour, home or form. To fulfil their assignment, the watchers must learn to read and use resources in nature, and eventually, the

watchers in Bäck's story identify the source of evil to the old mine and its
mistress, *Gruvfrun*, a powerful and treacherous female creature in Swedish
lore. In this case, the mistress of the local mine demands human sacrifice and
she keeps eighteen dead young men as hostages, *the walkers*, in her underworld
realm.

At the same time as Madeleine Bäck makes use of local folklore and history,
her trilogy explores and challenges the formula of today's young-adult and
crossover fiction about witches. As Maria Holmgren Troy finds characteristic
of what she calls Mats Strandberg and Sara B. Elfgren's *witch trilogy*, that
is, their Engelfors trilogy, Bäck employ a collective protagonist and shifting
focalisation.[15] Like Elfgren and Strandberg's trilogy, it is set in a mining town
characterised by post-industrial decline in the *rust belt* of Sweden and in a
region of where the persecution of witches were intense in the seventeenth
century. Like the teenage witches in Strandberg and Elfgren's Engelfors
trilogy, the young protagonists in Bäck's story gain access to powerful forces
of nature, and they depend on the guidance of an older woman, to handle
their new situation. However, in Bäck's trilogy, the place of evil is not located
to a socially defined place, such as the high school in Elfgren and Strandberg's
trilogy, but a space in the wilderness outside the village. Their mission is also
less clear and instead of being *the chosen ones*, the watchers are destined by
bloodline to participate in a battle between different powers of nature. The
established relationship between gender and duty is also contested. According
to what is known about the past in Bäck's Gästrikland triology, the walkers
have always been young men sacrificed by men belonging to families of
ironmasters. However, and in the present time of narration, the patrilineal
descent is broken; *Gruvfrun* is no longer pleased with man sacrifice carried out
by male ironmasters. Instead, she demands the sacrifice of a little girl, who
descends from a family of former ironmasters. In addition, the child is to be
offered not by her father but by another woman of the family, the girl's young
aunt. The only way to end the reign of *Gruvfrun* is to return the magic stone
found by Viktor in the local church but this time it must be returned by the
assistance of two female watchers. However, not only the patrilineal descent
of ironmasters but also the matrilineal descent of the watchers is broken in
the present time of narration. The inheritance of the old master watcher,
Gunhild, is passed on to her grandson Krister. Nevertheless, although born a
man, Krister is the most transgendered character in the novel. His emphatic
and healing qualities meet the requirements of being more powerful than an
ordinary watcher; he is recognised as a *Channakk*.

Although the reader does not know what will happen to the surviving
protagonists after they have defeated or escaped the power of *Gruvfrun*, they

seem to be united by respect and friendship independent of their families' past and their inherent qualities and assignments. In that way, Bäck's trilogy of *Gästrikland*, both demonstrates and challenges former patriarchal structures and a repressed matriarchal power structure related to ancient traditions with a clear link to nature and the local Swedish landscape. Therefore, it does not promote a clear polarisation between good and bad related to gender and untamed nature. For a start, the evil forces of nature appear in the shape of two young men: Victor, who falls victim to the powers of the magic stone and misuses it, and the man from the lake, who seduces and kills young women, such as Beata's bosom friend Celia. In addition, the local criminal gang also consists of a number of vicious male brutes, but in the end, when the source of pure evil is exposed, it emanates from a female creature of nature, *Gruvfrun*, who has been in control since people started mining in the region. What finally puts an end to her reign is that her gift to the ironmasters, the magic stone, is returned to her by the agency of female watchers, at the same time as her required offering of a little girl is stopped with the cost of the life of the female Master watcher. To be explicit, although some men might be powerful and in control of their business in Bäck's trilogy, the fundamental battle in nature between life and death is in the hands of female creatures and the agents of a repressed matriarchy. Furthermore, the ambivalent powers of nature and its local manifestations remain a mystery at the end of Bäck's trilogy.

Gendered and Transgressive Landscapes and Female Monsters

In Swedish Gothic, it is possible to distinguish between a Male and Female formula since the mid-nineteenth century in terms of plot, narrative technique, gendered focalisation and use of supernatural elements. The thematic focus in many Swedish stories concerns masculine and feminine identity and the nature of the family that shapes it, something William Patrick Day finds central to Gothic in general.[16] However, in the male version of Swedish Gothic there are few examples of that kind of transgressive male protagonists prepared to break social ethical norms in the quest for masculine fulfilment that Day finds characteristic of Gothic.[17] The Swedish male protagonist is more of a prey than a transgressor; he is an antihero or a hero of submission. Instead of emanating from his own nature, the threat is located to the female character and to a gendered and feminised landscape, in which the division between self and Other is unstable and blurred. The source of fear is a feminine Other, a dark power linked to untamed nature and a pre-Christian order or history.

It is also possible to identify a Swedish version of Female Gothic about women's confinement and their search of identity. Nonetheless, the Swedish version of Female Gothic differs from what Ellen Moer identified as the Anglo-American *travelling heroinism*, originated from Ann Radcliffe's heroines in flight from male abusers in Gothic environments in their search of lost mothers in their quest for self-definition.[18] Nor do the female protagonists of Swedish Gothic share those traits that characterise those victimised virtuous young women with passive obedience to male authority that Day identifies as a central Gothic theme.[19]

In the Swedish version of Female Gothic, the main threat is not a male tyrant and his Gothic domain but a danger located either in nature or in the female protagonist's own family history. On the one hand, the female protagonist is just as confined to the private world of her family as most Gothic heroines. On the other hand, her search for an absent mother or a female role model is a quest for a lost matriarchal society or for restabilising a new world order. In young-adult fiction, the utopian society is primarily a matriarchal world in line with today's ecofeminism.[20] However, in stories for adults and cross-over literature, such as *April Witch* and Bäck's *Gästrikland* trilogy, the new world is not a matriarchy based only on biological sex but rather on traditional feminine ideology. The heroines and their male allies are equipped with both transgressive and magic powers, and their main trials are to learn to control and use their double-edged talents in a positive way according to traditional female ideology. What once was the subversive theme of Female Gothic is now the explicit message, in particular in today's crossover fiction.

However, in both Male and Female Gothic, the Swedish landscape and local folklore play a significant part. In many male writers' and directors' stories, the threat is associated with a gendered and feminine wilderness, a scheming landscape populated by mythological female nature beings from Swedish folklore. In stories by women, however, untamed nature is often depicted as a positive resource of magic power and control, in particular in order to re-establish social and moral order. In Swedish Gothic, there might not be a gendered Gothic formula in accordance with what is recognised as Female and Male Gothic in Anglo-American literature and film. Instead, there is a gendered landscape and wilderness, as well as a male and female way of exploring local popular belief and the associated ideas of magic, from the mid-nineteenth century until the present day.

Chapter 3

NORDIC NOIR AND GOTHIC CRIMES

Since the millennium, Nordic crime stories have been widely consumed around the globe. They are often set in a bleak Nordic landscape and narrated from an afflicted detective's point of view, whose investigation exposes a morally complex society beneath the seemingly peaceful social surface of the Nordic welfare state. The popularity of these crime novels – sometimes called the *Nordic Noir* or the *Scandi Noir* – has given rise to adaptations and transnational fame. Stieg Larsson's Millennium trilogy (2005–7) and Henning Mankell's series about the Swedish police detective Kurt Wallander (1991–2013) have resulted in a number of Swedish and internationally produced films and TV series. The popularity of Nordic Noir is also due to several internationally successful TV series, such as the Danish *The Killing* (*Forbrydelsen*, 2007–12) and the Danish-Swedish *The Bridge* (*Broen/Bron*, 2011–18). The two TV series have given rise to several international productions. While the first one has resulted in an American version titled *The Killing* from 2011–14, the second one has inspired one French-British TV series, *The Tunnel* (2013–18) and one American adaptation, *The Bridge* (2013–14).

In the last two decades, a Gothic version of Nordic Noir has emerged that could be called Gothic crime in literature, film and TV productions. Within a realistic tradition of Nordic crime fiction, the police procedure is obstructed by apparently supernatural activities and the interference of uncanny characters. Beyond the well-known everyday world, a mythological world and a dark past appear to be operating and Gothic tropes and narrative strategies are used to mystify the background and the consequences of the committed crime. Although the crime mystery is eventually solved, the potential existence of supernatural powers is confirmed rather than negated. One of the most internationally awarded Swedish novelists of the genre hybridity is Johan Theorin with his quartet of Gothic crime novels set on the island of Öland in the Baltic Sea: *Echoes from the Dead* (*Skumtimmen*, 2007), *The Darkest Room* (*Nattfåk*, 2008), *The Quarry* (*Blodläge*, 2010) and *The Voices Beyond* (*Rörgast*, 2013). Another example is Cecilia Ekbäck's historical novels *Wolf Winter* (*I vargavinterns land*, 2015) and *In the Month of the Midnight Sun* (*Midnattssolens time*,

2016), both of which were first published in England. Both Ekbäck's novels and Måns Mårlind and Björn Stein's Swedish-French TV drama *Midnight Sun* (*Midnattssolens time/Jour polaire*, 2016) are set in the most remote part of northern Sweden and describe the conflicts between the settling Swedes and the indigenous population of Sámi people. In addition, TV series, such as Henrik Björn's *Soil Sprouts* (*Jordskott*, 2015) and Johan Kindblom and Thomas Tivemark's *Ängelby* (*Ängelby*, 2015), are examples of Gothic crime stories located on the outskirts of urban civilisation, in areas challenging the ideals of today's Swedish society. Both *Soil Sprouts* and *Ängelby* revolve around the mystery of a missing child and in what way the disappearance is entangled with seemingly supernatural elements trying to protect the local forest and the local community at large against external commercial interests.

The subgenre of Gothic crime is far from new; it revives a tradition going back to the mid-nineteenth century. In that way, Swedish literature convincingly demonstrates what several scholars have claimed: the Gothic genre gave rise to detective fiction.[1] In, for example, Carl Jonas Love Almqvist's *Skällnora Mill* (*Skällnora qvarn*, 1838) and Zacharias Topelius' *A Night and a Morning* (*En natt och en morgon*, 1843) a whodunit-plot is combined with supernatural happenings and a Gothic setting. As demonstrated elsewhere, both stories are set in remote locations in the countryside and are structured as the male protagonist's journey into a nightmarish desolate location of mystery, where the strange behaviour of the local inhabitants adds to the atmosphere, at the same time as their conduct, in combination with local customs, obstructs the protagonist's quest for truth.[2] Although the male detective tries to solve a suspected murder case, he is not in control of the investigation and he does not arrive at a satisfying solution. On the narrative level, unreliable narrators and distorted viewpoints make the distinction between reality and imagination dissolve and leave the readers in a state of ambiguity. Especially in *Skällnora Mill*, the reader is led astray; the reader is left with the question whether a murder was ever committed, or if the crime was a rumour fabricated by a malicious man, or if most of the events depicted just took place in the first-person narrator's hallucinogen imagination.

Today's Gothic crime demonstrates a similar mix of Gothic and realistic narration. The crime investigation exposes a complex relationship between location, time and focalisation but in today's stories, local mythology, ancient traditions and conceptions of supernatural creatures even more activate hidden crimes and repressed memories of a dark past. Although the detective eventually comes up with a solution and the murderer is exposed, there might still be parts of the mystery that are never clarified. In Johan Theorin's Öland quartet series, for example, the realistic depiction of the modern crime investigation together with seemingly supernatural happenings generate a narrative that activates ancient concepts and a repressed past. At the beginning of the stories, supernatural forces connected to the past of Öland seem to be the cause of the killing. However – and as argued elsewhere – during the crime investigation, the terror is not located in the past but in the present.[3] Compared to the evil drives behind the present murder, the wrongdoings in the past are reduced to ill-fated coincidences or unfortunate accidents rather than scheming plans of evil by a selfish and malicious mind. The true terror and crime in Theorin's Öland quartet is the transgression of modern commercial aspects of free tourist enterprise and the ways in which greed turns people into lawbreakers. The true offenders are always persons with commercial ambitions, who are prepared to use all means to exploit both the local landscape and its people.

Even more representative of today's Gothic crime and its way of addressing topical subjects are Björn's TV series *Soil Sprouts* and Cecilia Ekbäck's novels *Wolf Winther* and *In the Month of the Midnight Sun*. Like Theorin's Öland quartet, they are place-focused stories, in which the setting plays a significant role. In the first season of *Soil Sprouts*, the disappearances of children seem to be tangled with the conflicts between obscure elements striving to protect the old-growth forest and the neighbouring community that depend on the planned expansion of the local timber and mining industry. Also in Ekbäck's novels, the location is fundamental to the plot. Both novels are set in the endless wilderness in the north of Sweden, at Svartåsen Mountain in the Lapland region. While the first novel takes place in winter in the early eighteenth century, the second one is set in mid-summer in the mid-nineteenth century. In both cases, the newly arrived protagonists act as amateur detectives to investigate the killings of some settlers and the crime investigation unearth dark secrets in Swedish history. Like many Gothic crime stories of today, the TV series *Soil Sprouts* and Ekbäck's Svartåsen series address topical environmental issues, at the same time as they heavily draw on Norse mythology and local folklore.

Drawing on genre theory in combination with an intersectional focus on power relations, this chapter explores two representative examples of recent Gothic crime, the first season of Henrik Björn's TV series *Soil Sprouts* (2015) and Cecilia Ekbäck's novel *In the Month of the Midnight Sun* (2016). It demonstrates the distinctive features of Swedish Gothic crime and its blend of Gothic mystery and the formula of a modern crime investigation in order to address current issues. In particular, it probes in what way the depiction of a haunted Gothic space, in combination with the use of old conceptions of supernatural powers, is employed to uncover a dark part of Swedish history and the shady preconditions for today's industrialised welfare society.

Crime by Nature

In Henrik Björn's TV series *Soil Sprouts*, the viewer is from the beginning placed in a position of hesitation. Like in Mark Frost and David Lynch's *Twin Peaks*, the forest provides a palpable and living presence throughout the series.[4] On the one hand, the story is set in a recognisable contemporary Swedish environment; on the other hand, the crime investigation transports the audience into an arboreal place of mystery, secret signs and popular belief. In the first season, police detective Eva Thörnblad (Moa Gammel) leaves Stockholm to visit her hometown of Silverhöjd to deal with the death and probate of her late father Johan Thörnblad (Lars-Erik Berenett) and his large timber felling and processing business, Thörnblad Mineral & Cellulosa. Her private reason to return is to investigate the disappearance of a local boy as she sees similarities between his disappearance and that of her daughter Josefine (Amie Vestholm). Seven years ago, six-year-old Josefine disappeared beside a lake in the forest and the official explanation was that she drowned. However, the body was never found and Eva believes that her daughter was abducted and that the same kidnapper is behind the disappearance of the boy. Soon, Eva teams up with the chief detective from the Department of National Operations, Göran Wass (Göran Rangerstam) and the local police detective Tom Aronsson (Richard Forsgren).

When Eva leaves her professional and urban life in the Swedish capital, she moves into a magical world of what James Donaghy has called *fairytale-noir*.[5] Shot from above, she is seen driving her car on endless roads in a Nordic landscape of desolate misty woodlands. In twilight, she arrives at her father's mansion in Silverhöjd, where a black raven lurks and wind chimes made of silver forks are tolling outside the entrance. When she enters the hall, the light is blown, at the same time as family portrays and deer trophies on the walls add to the Gothic atmosphere. When Eva finds a picture of her daughter, she is transposed to the day the girl went missing. In a flashback, the little girl dressed in a fair summer dress is seen playing by the lake in the forest, while Eva walks away a couple of steps to pick up a blanket. When Eva turns around, the girl is gone without making any sound or leaving any traces behind.

Repeatedly, the distinction between past and present, memory and current reality is blurred in the series. Often, the audience cannot trust what is shown on the screen, if it is what really happens or if it is a distorted version of Eva's perception or memories. When she one night has a car accident, it first appears to be caused by a hallucination. All of a sudden, a spectral form appears in front of the car, which makes Eva brake and drive off the road. When she comes to and starts searching, she cannot find anyone or anything. Then all of a sudden, she distinguishes a ghost-like version of a young girl in a catatonic state. An earring in one of the girl's ears convinces Eva that it must be her lost daughter Josefin. However, when the zombie-like girl is brought to the hospital, there is no earring to be found and a DNA test proves that Eva and the girl are not genetically related. Still Eva is convinced of the identity of the girl. When she starts singing a song she used to sing for her baby daughter, the seemingly unconscious girl wakes up and starts humming the tune. Sometime later, the girl escapes from the hospital in a more or less miraculous way. Later she turns up in Eva's old mansion, where Eva starts nursing her in secret. Although the girl seems to be Eva's lost daughter, her lifeform is dubious. The tests run at the hospital indicate that she is infected by some kind of parasite. By the audience, she has also been seen leaving her bed to put her hand into the soil of a flowerpot, something that seems to change her fingers into tendrils and roots. When Eva later tries to feed her, she refuses to eat. At the same time, some unknown person or creature delivers bottles to the mansion with strange content, which the girl devours. Thus, her otherness and unhuman character is progressively proved to the audience.

Soil Sprouts is an example of Gothic crime, in which the modern crime investigation enhances its Gothic qualities. Because of her professional work as a police officer, Eva is drawn into a strange and menacing chain of events related to a crime, and because she is a police officer, she investigates them accordingly. The inquiry into the disappearance of the boy triggers a series of killings, as well as seemingly supernatural activities connected to the forest and its lakes. At the same time as the recently committed crimes and their complications keep Eva and the local team busy, the landscape – the forests and its lakes and rocks – is set up as the main character and a scheming antagonist in its own right. Gradually, Eva's investigation proves that the forest and the activities in the present time of narration are linked to her family history and her ancestors, who started to commercialise nature with their lumber industry in the eighteenth century. When Eva starts to reconstruct her father's last years in life and what killed him, she is left with various contradictory pieces of information. At a specific place in the forest, which is linked to several weird happenings, she discovers an entrance to an underground passageway ending up in the cellar of her mansion. In a secret room in the attic of the mansion, she finds ancient sealed contracts and maps of the region. On videotapes left in her father's room, her father has recorded his physical decline and information of his death. When Eva approaches the former local detective Olof Gran (Hans Mosesson), who investigated the missing of her daughter, he behaves strangely and seems to be obsessed with studying ancient documents on the local history of Silverhöjd. He also tells her, that what happened probably originated in that her father 'had fallen out with the forest'. Later on, he gives her a warning: 'Once nature gets hold of you it will never let go of you.'[6] In addition, outside the supermarket, Eva meets a bag-lady-looking woman, Ylva (Vanja Blomkvist), who offers her a tin, because she 'needs it'.[7] Although Eva refuses to accept the tin, she finds it later on her doorstep and when she opens the lid, she finds it contains a greenish, revolting smelling paste.

To viewers familiar with Nordic folklore, certain traces found in the forest indicate that Silverhöjd is a troll habitat. The viewer is also presented with signs on logs and pieces of old paper that looks like *troll runes*, old Nordic letters used as spells in rituals. The disappearances of the children and the return of the catatonic Josefine also remind of folktales about trolls and changelings. Trolls are known from Nordic folklore to be ugly, stupid and humanlike creatures living in the wilderness, in the dark forest or in high mountains, where they hold enormous treasures of mineral and stones. They crave for beautiful human children, and therefore they are prone to snatch babies and replace them with their broods. If a kidnapped person succeeds to escape, he or she returns as a different being, neither human nor troll. The homecomer is doomed to eternal estrangement and alienation, according to Swedish myths. At the same time as the audience is reminded of troll mythology, the crime investigation in *Soil Sprouts* progressively exposes the existences of trolls and other forest entities. Furthermore, the modern technical methods and forensics demonstrated in the series confirm the otherness of these creatures and changelings. Although the found girl probably is Eva's daughter Josefine, she has changed into another creature or species suffering from a parasite that has changed her deoxy ribose nucleic acid (DNA). Like trolls in folktales, she cannot digest human food but only consume soil-based raw products, in this case bottled *Essence of Forest*. In this manner, she demonstrates an extreme example of what Stacy Alaimo terms trans-corporeality, that the human body is intermeshed with the environment and non-human nature.[8]

The crime investigation does not only confirm the existence of humanlike creatures known from Swedish folklore. Progressively, Eva and her team discover that the children's disappearance is inextricably tangled with the prospected expansion of Thörnblad Mineral & Cellulosa and the initiated blasting in the forest in order to find a new ore body of silver. As Irina Souch points out, the juxtaposition of different shots in the series progressively redirects the viewer's attention and suggests that the wrongdoings in the present are linked to the ecocide in the past.[9] Corporate greed and its effects, such as green undrinkable water, motivate local environmentalists to demonstrate in order to stop the blasting and the destruction of old-growth forest. At the same time as the industrial activities provoke the supernatural powers and creatures of the forest, the members of the board of the Thörnblad industry are taking extra precautions in order to protect their children, indicating that they know more about the disappearances than they want to communicate to the police. When Eva finds old documents in her father's secret chamber in the mansion, she comes across an explanation of the seemingly supernatural activities. In the eighteenth century, her ancestor signed a contract, in which he and his family for all future promised to leave and protect certain areas of the forest, areas that belong to its inhabitants, the indigenous species of human-like creatures living underground. When Eva's father applied the current technique of pesticide spraying in 1978, he broke the contract and his transgression killed everybody living in the forest except one infant, which the old woman Ylva found, nursed and named Muns. When Thörnblad Cellulose & Mineral once more breaks the pact, the pit-dwelling Muns starts acting to avenge the killing of his people by abducting the board members' children one by one. In that way, Muns provides a powerful imagery of the pact in the past and its inescapable historical legacies.

The ecological message of the series *Soil Sprouts* is clear. When Eva learns about her father's breach of contract, she realises that his pesticide spraying of the forest has provoked its only surviving creature, Muns, to fight back. The effects of her father's transgression confirm a system of Old Testament justice that means that the sins of the fathers are visited on their children. Because of the contract breach, the members of the Thörnblad family are all suffering the brunt of their ancestors' exploitation of the forest; a wood parasite consumed Johan and the same parasite is growing inside Josefine. After being fatally injured, Eva is also infected with the parasite *Jordskott*, although she learns to control it and benefits from its side effects, such as her sharpened senses. Together with her colleague Göran Wass, she tries to stop those persons who out of greed or hate try to exterminate the local population of supernatural or unhuman species. However, the true criminal or real parasite in Silverhöjd is not separate individuals but humankind as such and its reckless violation of nature and its indigenous population of supernatural beings for profit, in this case, the extraction of silver.

Besides the ecological – and to some extent postcolonial – subject, the most central theme of *Jordskott* is parental anguish and love, a theme progressively frequent and developed in today's Swedish fiction. In the first scene of the series, its prologue, Eva is introduced as a negotiator and police officer trying to stop a desperate man from shooting his wife, who he is holding hostage in a bid to win back custody of his daughter. After Eva's move to Silverhöjd, the audience is introduced to several other cases of parental distress: several local parents' agony when their young children go missing, the detective Tom's longing for his autistic daughter Ida (Mira Gustafsson), Gerda Gunnarsson's (Lia Boysen) untiring nursing of her retarded son Nicklas (Henrik Knutsson) and Eva's persistent efforts to bring back her daughter Josefine. In addition, the old woman Ylva's bond to the raving avenger and last survivor of the alien people of the forest, the troll Muns, is an example of unconditional maternal love. Another and more clearly negative example of parental agony is the main human culprit, the bounty hunter Harry Storm (Ville Virtanen), who finds himself assigned to eliminate all connected with the forest out of revenge because he once lost his son.

However, the two most extraordinary cases of parental anguish are Gerda and Eva, both of whom are prepared to trade anything and anyone for their dysfunctional children. The frightening message of the TV drama is not only the environmental effects of human pollution but also the length a parent – in particular a mother – is prepared to go for her child regardless of the future consequences for her as a person or for humankind as such. Both Eva and Gerda are prepared to bleed the forest dry for silver or other substances to secure the future of their children. If Wass and his secret society is ruled by the motto *naturam vita nostra tuemur* that is, 'with our lives we protect' referring to the wilderness and its creatures, the same motto means to Gerda and Eva with our lives we protect our biological children, no matter its means or effects on other individuals, humankind or the planet as such. In the end, the audience is left in ambiguity about the true nature of motherhood and/or its monstrosity.

Racialised Space

While *Jordskott* revolves around the themes of ecological and parental anguish, Cecilia Ekbäck's two novels *Wolf Winther* and *In the Month of the Midnight Sun* demonstrate a new tendency in Gothic crime, to employ a historical setting in order to activate repressed memories of a hidden Nordic past. The novels are located in the arctic wilderness in northern Sweden in the Lapland region. In both novels, the story is presented through mediation of three characters, one who is familiar with the location and the community since several years and two characters who have newly arrived to the Swedish settlement at Blackåsen Mountain. However, the crime and its investigation are central to the plot in the novels, in particular in the second novel. In *In the Month of the Midnight Sun*, the Minister of Justice in Stockholm sends out his foster son and son-in-law, the mineralogist Magnus Stille, because there has been a massacre in Lapland; a man of the nomadic Sámi people has killed three men in the parsonage: a clergyman, a law enforcement officer and an unnamed settler. Although Magnus Stille's official mission is to prospect the iron ore deposit of Blackåsen Mountain, his true assignment is to investigate the crime. On his journey in the summer of 1856, he is required to bring his young sister-in-law,

Lovisa Rosenblad, who is sent away from home in disgrace by her father. The happenings are focalised from Magnus's and Lovisa's viewpoints, together with the viewpoint of an old Sámi woman, Biijá/Ester, who has just lost her husband and because of that has decided to stay at her people's winter camp at Blackåsen Mountain instead of accompanying her tribe and their reindeers up on the fell.

The crime investigation in *In the Month of the Midnight Sun* is more in line with professional detective work than in Ekbäck's previous novel. Although Magnus has to work undercover and he and Lovisa arrive at the region of Lapland several weeks after the manslaughters were committed, he questions the suspected and imprisoned Sámi man and all witnesses he meets on their way to Blackåsen Mountain. He tries to find possible motives behind the killings and he does not believe that the old Sámi man in custody has been able to kill three younger men by himself. When he and Lovisa arrive at Blackåsen Village, he examines the crime scene and tries to interrogate the villagers. Because the settlers are unwilling to talk about what happened, the assistance of Lovisa becomes vital to Magnus. As a woman, she has access to the female community of the settlement; she is invited to the dead clergy-man's and the constable's wives. She is also let in by the haughty Adelaide, who now is the only survivor of the village counsel and who had a long and close relationships with the three killed men. A crime that at first appears to be committed by a maniac in a fit of rage turns out to be an act linked to a number of wrongdoings that are connected to Blackåsen Mountain and the settlers' relations to the local Sámi community. At the same time as Magnus and Lovisa uncover the intricate and dark history of the settlement, they find themselves progressively influenced by and linked to the mountain and its uncanny history.

Compared to the first novel, *Wolf Winter*, the setting of *In the Month of the Midnight Sun* is more distinctly concentrated on Blackåsen Mountain, partly because the population of the Swedish settlers has grown and the village has moved closer to the mountain, partly because Magnus's mission as a min-eralogist is to map and investigate the geology of the mountain for future mining. Like in the first novel, the mountain is from the beginning depicted as a brutal and unforgiving space, where supernatural powers connected to the Sámi culture seep into the harsh lives of the settlers. When it is first pre-sented to Magnus, it is as 'the most gruesome of places'.[10] The maps of the region kept in Stockholm are missing and on the rough map that Magnus finds when he arrives at the closest town to the mountain, Luleå, it is marked with symbols that he first identifies as 'blonde curls on painted angels', but later discovers are devil's horns.[11] Also from the point of view of the Sámi woman Biijá/Ester, it is depicted as an ominous place of ancient Sámi cults.

It was at the mountain her late husband Nila/Nils first qualified to become a shaman – *Noaidi* – and it was at the mountain he annually used to sacrifice to the spirits of the mountain.

Progressively, the mountain becomes a character in its own right that affects the doings of the protagonists, their drives and moods in different ways. When Biijá/Ester and Lovisa accompany Magnus on his expeditions to map the mountain, they constantly feel the presence of a dark power looming at the place. From Biijá/Ester's animistic viewpoint, the mountain is alive; it transpires in the sunshine and it feels awkward when Magnus starts to examine it: 'He strips it, embarrasses it.'[12] When Lovisa alone first approaches the mountain, she finds a labyrinth with stones, but when she tries to find its entrance, she is stopped by falling stones and she falls and hurts herself. At the same time, she knows she is watched and hears a voice in her head and thinks: 'Don't let them see you are frightened, I think, uncertain as to whom "they" might refer.'[13] When Magnus starts digging to expose the banded ore formation, he is almost killed by a falling rock.

Magnus's mapping of Blackåsen Mountain exposes the dark history of the place. The killing in the present time of narration is linked to what happened some decades earlier, when the present members of the village counsel were young and violated the Sámi labyrinth of cult. After their transgression, the young men seemed to start to act under the influence of evil spirits. One of them killed his father, for which he was sentenced to prison. The other three men raped a young girl, while their female friend Adelaide was forced to watch. Nobody was ever legally punished for the rape but they are all more or less traumatised by what happened. To stop the bad influence of the mountain and its evil spirits, the late village vicar called in the local Sámi shaman, Nila/Nils, whose ceremonial proceedings to break the revenge of the mountain doomed the partakers to infertility and childlessness.

Although three settlers are killed because of the gold find in the mountain, the real trigger of evil is the disclosure of their violation of the Sámi cult place and the sexual abuse of the girl. The knowledge of their crimes in the past appears to endow the killer with supernatural powers beyond human control. The same powers that operated behind the killings of the three men seem to come alive once more in the novel: when the organiser of the three killings is caught and kept in custody. Later when Magnus returns to the room, he finds the wrongdoer punished by a violent death although the two persons who was assigned to guard the evildoer – Lovisa and Biijá/Ester – cannot explain what really happened. Yet, Magnus detects certain uncanny similarities between the killings of the three men and the one who planned the killings. Still no rational or trustworthy explanation is presented in Ekbäck's novel. In the end, Magnus finds himself unable to make sense of what has happened, something he blames himself for because he is suffering from insomnia due to the merciless midnight sun. That is, he finds himself too exhausted to be able to think clearly.

Thus, in *In the Month of the Midnight Sun*, the crime investigation progressively exposes conflicts between the Swedish settlers and the indigenous population of the Sámi people. Thereby it exposes a shady side of Swedish colonial history, something that is both repressed and tabooed. As part of the nation building from the early seventeenth century onwards, the Swedish state encouraged colonisation of the land that was used for reindeer herding by the Sámi people in northern Sweden. At the same time, the Swedish church began missionary work and the Sámi belief, which comprised animism, polytheism and shamanism, come under attack. In Ekbäck's novel, the crime and its Gothic features are primarily connected to the organised colonisation of the Sámi people and the repression of their religion. As normally by Swedes in the nineteenth century, the indigenous population in the novel is referred to as *Lapps*, a term that nowadays is regarded as offensive by some Sámi people. They are also repeatedly characterised by the local Swedish authorities as a primitive people, and it is repeatedly demonstrated in the novel that the Swedish settlers do not respect the Sámi culture and the Sámi people's way of life as nomadic reindeer herders. In that way, the novel expresses a racial anxiety presumed to exist in the Swedish nineteenth-century society. From Biijá/Ester's viewpoint, the oppressive Christianisation of her people is described and in what way the Sámi population is prescribed to use Christian names, that is, Biijá is by the Swedish authorities baptised Ester and her husband Nila is named Nils.

To the two newcomers, Magnus and Lovisa, the investigation of the crime is a confrontation with social control, racism and otherness. Their inquiry does not only reveal the systematic oppression of the Sámi people; it also exposes their own family history and their ties to the region. In particular to the orphaned Magnus, the self-knowledge comes at a bitter cost. He has to confront his nightmare of repressed memories and childhood trauma when he learns about his Sámi origin. Since childhood, his face is split in two halves; the right side is handsome and commands respect, while his left side is scared and disgusting. His twofold face mirrors his dual identity; his official social status as a high-status geologist belonging to the family of the Swedish Minister of Justice, contra his repressed biological Sámi inheritance and racialised otherness. His origin has been kept from him until Lovisa shares the dying minister Axel Bring's confession with him at the very end of their stay. In one way, Magnus embodies what Judith Halberstam identifies as a Gothic skin show, an external representation of monstrosity and horror related to certain skins, external features and deviant bodies. In that way, he represents what Halberstam, drawing on Sigmund Freud, calls a repressed foreign body that stores up fearful memories of traumas in the past.[14] Still Magnus does not become an example of a male monster or transgressor; he does not give in to his external monstrosity, nor does he submit to the racial implications of his genetic origin. To him, the crime investigation discloses the tyranny of racism and he refuses to define persons or be defined himself according to biological categories at the sacrifice of culture and social status. Although he returns to Stockholm afflicted by the truth about his origin and his family history, he does it as the geologist Magnus Stille, and as a member of the family of the Swedish Minister of Justice.

Also to Lovisa, the stay at Blackåsen Mountain leads to an inner journey and revaluation of her true nature and destiny. Her meeting with the dying Axel Bring, who once knew her father, has made her revise her painful relationship with her father. Contrary to Magnus, she has no inherent biological connection with the Sámi population or the mountain. Still she immediately adapts to the location and the midnight sun. Unlike Magnus, she sleeps better than ever in the nights of midnight sun, and she seems to develop an eerie connection to the Sámi community and its members. To Biijá/Ester's surprise, for example, she calls Nila/Nils by his Sámi name without being told it. She is also only one who is sensitive to the dead shaman's spiritual presence and willpower.

Despite being dead, the presence of the former Sámi shaman Nila/Nils haunts the characters in Ekbäck's novel. From Biijá/Ester's point of view, the reader is progressively told about her late husband's fearful vision, after which he carved out the face of the killer. Because of his ongoing practice of shamanism, the Sámi tribe sentenced him to exclusion and death for fear of reprisals by the Swedish authorities. Still, the dead Nila/Nils is an agent in the story and text. In embedded short passages set in italics, the voice of him breaks through and the only one he is able to reach is Lovisa. In the first passage, when he approaches her in her sleep, he compares her to the mountain: 'You are open like a mountain rift. Many would step straight in, but I won't. I will talk and hope you listen. [...] My name is Nila and I need you to hear my story. Can you hear me?'[15] Lovisa does hear him, which is recurrently confirmed by her actions, in particular in connection to the confrontation with and death of the person, who is behind the first three killings. Although the investigation of the crimes is concluded, and the reader is presented with a satisfying explanation, many questions remain to be answered about the murders and about Lovisa's and Magnus's contributions. In that way, Ekbäck's novel ends as an example of what David Punter calls *paranoiac fiction*, which places the reader in a position of doubts and uncertainty.[16] In the end and in the very last passage of the novel, the reader is left with the echo of the dead Nila/Nils's voice once more trying to reach the living, this time to summon not Lovisa but Magnus.

Violation of Nature and Inhabitants

Henrik Björn's TV drama *Soil Spouts* and Cecilia Ekbäck's novel *In the Month of the Midnight Sun* are good representatives of today's Gothic crime, that is, a Gothic subgenre of Nordic Noir where the crime investigation is obstructed by seemingly supernatural elements linked to the Nordic landscape and its past. The interventions of supernatural events offer an alternative structure of cause and effect that makes the audience reconsider the motives behind the crime, and sometimes even the nature of the phenomenological world as such. Thus, the stories are also examples of the kind of Gothic that Fred Botting, referring to Foucault, has identified as a heterotopian form and counter-site of utopia, where the dominant structuring principles of the reflected milieu are all at once 'represented, contested and inverted'.[17] At the same time, the desire to explain and understand the mystery is made explicit through the protagonists' work as investigating detective that seeks answers. In *Soil Sprouts*, the crime investigation exposes the ecological effects of humankind and the accelerating industrial exploitation of the forest and mountain of Silverhöjd, which was initiated when the police detective Eva Thörnblad's ancestor in the eighteenth century started his timber and mineral industry. In *In the Month of the Midnight Sun*, the amateur detective Magnus Stille's official mission is to map Svartåsen Mountain in order to initiate extraction of minerals and an industrial exploitation of a landscape that has belonged to and been used by the local Sámi population for reindeer herding. In both stories, the crime investigation uncovers the ongoing repression of an indigenous population closely connected to the local area: the mythical nature beings living beneath the forest in the pit in *Soil Sprouts* and the Sámi population in *In the Month of the Midnight Sun*.

Like in most Gothic crime, the ecological message is explicit in Björn's TV drama and Ekbäck's novel. Both stories revolve around the idea of nature's revenge. Instead of catching the culprit and arriving at a satisfying solution, the crime investigation exposes a complex course of events beyond the simplistic laws of cause and effect. In the end, it reveals that the true wrongdoer is not a single murderer but humankind as such and its violation of the landscape and natural resources. In both stories, the intent to map and extract minerals results in devastating effects on the local ecological system and the associate cultural landscape. Ekbäck's Blackåsen novels also demonstrate a new tendency in Swedish Gothic crime, to employ a historical setting in order to activate repressed memories of a hidden Nordic past. *In the*

Month of the Midnight Sun, the crime investigation exposes the psychological and social processes caused by the colonisation of Sámpi, both among the Swedish settlers and the Sámi population. In that way, Ekbäck's novel presents what Rebecca Duncan in relation to postcolonial issues calls a *creative dissent*, a rejection of obvious state of affairs in order to demonstrate that things are more complex and entangled than they first appear.[18] In this specific case, Ekbäck explores the painful aspects of the Christianisation of the Sámi population and the Swedish authorities and settlers' exorcism of an ancient world view marked by mythical creatures and magic powers.

In addition, *Soil Sprouts* explores another recurrent theme in today's Swedish fiction, the cherished biological and mental bond between parent and child. It is an example of a *creative dissent* that examines the negative aspects of parental love. The most fear-provoking and taboo-breaking theme in the TV drama is the length a parent is prepared to go for his or her biological child regardless of the consequences for other people, and the ecological system of the planet. In particular, two mothers, Eva Thörnblad and Gerda Gunnarsson, demonstrate the ruthless side of maternal love, and that they are willing to give up everything and everybody to save their children. In Björn's TV drama, the true evildoer and monster is human nature, in particular the negative, possessive and egoistic, aspects of parental love.

Chapter 4

SWEDISH GOTHIC: DARK FORCES OF THE WILDERNESS

As demonstrated above, there is a long Gothic tradition in Swedish literature and film. It goes back to the Romantic period and the early nineteenth century when the first phase of imported English and German stories inspired Swedish writers to modify and adapt Gothic conventions to their local audiences. From the beginning, Swedish Gothic were place-focused stories, in which the Nordic landscape takes the role of a labyrinthine Gothic castle as a space of fear and terror. At the same time, the Swedish version of Gothic was densely intertextual with explicit references to well-known and iconic works produced outside Scandinavia. Thereby, Swedish writers placed themselves in a tradition of transnational Gothic, at the same time as they took for granted that their audiences were genre-aware and recognised references to iconic works. The first Swedish vampire story, Viktor Rydberg's *The Vampire* (1848), is an extended and elaborated response to Polidori's story from 1819, while Aurora Ljungstedt's *The House of the Devil* (1853) is a Gothic novel in the style of Ann Radcliffe and with explicit references to Radcliffe's novels.

Also, today's Swedish writers and filmmakers place themselves in a global Gothic tradition of canonised novels and films. The impact of international blockbusters, such as *Blair Witch Project*, has resulted in a domesticated Scandinavian version of mockumentaries with distinct Nordic features. The films are often structured as a journey from the ordinary urban everyday world into a mythological world lurking outside or beyond modern society. Here the force of nature acts as an external monstrous antagonist, such as in *The Unknown* (2000), directed by Michael Hjorth. In addition, a certain kind of Swedish blend of Gothic and realist narration has gained widespread international acclaim. One of the earliest and most successful examples is John Ajvide Lindqvist's bestselling vampire novel *Let the Right One In* (2007). It is set in a recognisable and explicitly named suburb outside the Swedish capital Stockholm, and it combines social realism with supernatural elements to address topical social problems. It was immediately translated into English and about 20 other languages. Lindqvist was also asked to write the screenplay to Tomas Alfredson's Swedish film adaptation from 2008, while Matt Reeves American remake, *Let Me In*, was released in 2010.

The most striking feature of Swedish Gothic since the early nineteenth century is the central part played by the Nordic landscape and mythological creatures of nature known from Nordic myths and popular belief. Untouched nature is portrayed as the monstrous other and can be equated with a character in its own right that attacks and transforms the human protagonist. In the male formula of Swedish Gothic, and in many stories by male writers and directors from the nineteenth century onwards, the Nordic scenery is a gendered landscape of forbidden passions. In Victor Rydberg's novel *Singoalla* (1857), the young Christian knight's meeting with a nomadic pagan girl triggers his sexual awaking. At the same time, it stirs up his innate violent passions and his repressed paternal family history about a progenitor that was known for his fervent worship of the ancient Norse gods. Also, today's afflicted male protagonists are submitted to a menacing world of animism and pre-Christian conceptions that evokes transgressions in the past that are connected with his family and its place-bound past, as in for example John Ajvide Lindqvist's *The Harbour* (2008). The characters' encounter with the dark history of the location is also – as in Tommy Wiklund and Sony Laguna's film *Wither* (2012) – depicted as an expression of cultural anxiety, primarily a fear of feminised wilderness and its threat to man-made structures and civilisation. In both cases, the male character is placed in a state of mental dissolution and chaos where no boundaries exist between past and present, inner and outer space, the self and the Nordic wilderness.

In the Swedish version of Female Gothic, women writers have often employed local mythology and supernatural interference to depict women's social confinement and struggle for individuality. Some early examples are Selma Lagerlöf's novels *Gösta Berling's Saga* (1891) and *A Manor House Tale* (1899). Since the millennium, old folktales of fear-provoking female creatures are frequently explored to address gender issues of persecution and social alienation. In her novel *April Witch* (1997), Majgull Axelson combines various myths about witches to confront certain aspects of the Swedish welfare system and its gendered preconceptions. Several writers have emphasised local traditions linked to Swedish history and Nordic mythology to modify the formula of young-adult and crossover fiction about witches and witchcraft. By using a collective protagonist and shifting focalisation, the importance of women's cooperation is accentuated; the young protagonists are only able to gain access to the powerful forces of nature – and thereby to fight the evil powers – if they do it together as a shared duty. In stories, such as Madeleine

Bäck's *Gästrikland* trilogy (2015–18), the protagonists' joint battle against the local Mistress of the old Mine both demonstrates and challenges the established patriarchal structures, as well as possible consequences of matriarchal sovereignty based on local traditions and the ambivalent powers of nature.

Thus, the role of the Nordic landscape has become increasingly ambivalent in today's Swedish Gothic. On the one hand, the Nordic wilderness is depicted as a remote, vicious and alien space that attacks and conquers human structures and society, and even the human mind. On the other hand, the role of the location and its creatures is multifaceted, in particular in today's troll fiction based on Nordic folklore about trolls, changelings and enchantment. Several writers and directors employ troll mythology to explore the kinship between trolls and humans and to address environmental issues of biological survival and social alienation, indigenous populations and endangered species. In folktales, trolls are primarily depicted from the human protagonist's perspective as primitive, dangerous and hostile humanoid beings. Therefore, their potential threat to the human characters is vital to the atmosphere of terror. However, in today's Gothic fiction, the anthropocentric viewpoint is challenged. In Stefan Spjut's novel *Stallo* (2012), the relationship between humans and trolls is multi-layered and the differences between humans and trolls are distressingly unclear. In John Ajvide Lindqvist's *Border* (2006) and Ali Abbasi's film adaptation from 2018, the distinction between human and troll is even more ambiguous. In Lindqvist's novella, the reader learns to know the humanised troll from her internal perspective in order to share her agony when she discovers her true nature and realises its consequences. Although her otherness is linked to her personal tragedy and biological nature of not being human, it also highlights a number of unsatisfactory circumstances in human society as such. From the troll's internal viewpoint, the essence of human nature and norms are confronted, in particular humans' ongoing abuse of nature, other species and lifeforms. The environmental message and the troll's otherness and social alienation are even more stressed in Abbassi's film. In it, the female troll comes to stand for both another species and an ethnic minority in Swedish society; her identity crisis is used to address both urgent environmental concerns and various postcolonial aspects of eugenic practices in Swedish history.

While the essence of being human is examined in contemporary troll fiction, various aspects of the foundation of the Swedish welfare state are confronted in today's Gothic crime stories. In these stories, the crime investigation is obstructed by seemingly supernatural elements in order to expose hidden parts of a Swedish history related to environmental exploitation, colonisation and racism. Most such stories are located in sparsely populated areas on the outskirts of modern urban society, as in for example Henrik Björn's TV series *Soil Sprouts* (2015), or in a historical setting, as in Ceclia Ekbäck's novel *In the Month of the Midnight Sun* (2016). In both cases, the crime investigation exposes an uncanny connection between time and location, the past and the present. The local scene is set up as a potent antagonist to the detective's request for information. Simultaneously, the presence and interference of the surrounding landscape make the detective discover transgressions in the past of significance to the present offences. Despite the fact that the crime is finally solved, some peculiarities are never rationally explained. The existence of supernatural phenomena beyond human control is rather confirmed than negated by the crime investigation. However, the interference of uncanny powers does not only enhance the Gothic qualities of the crime story; it also exposes the true evildoer. That is, the root of the evil is always human nature as such, and, in particular, humans' reckless abuse and exploitation of natural resources. As in most Swedish Gothic of today, the true monster is the anthropocentric view on the environment and its local indigenous populations, no matter if it is another ethnic minority, species or lifeform. We humans are not only guilty of suppression and extinction; our worst felony is that we have dispatched all unsympathetic beings and prior populations to another dimension of our anthropocentric reality, the world of myth and folktales.

To conclude, in today's Swedish Gothic, the distinction between human and untamed nature is markedly ambiguous. The wilderness is progressively acting against the protagonists through specific representatives, often well-known mythological figures from Nordic folklore, such as witches and trolls. The landscape and its seemingly supernatural beings do not primarily endanger the characters' physical existence and doings by preventing them from reaching their goals. Instead, the hostile powers of nature act by invading, controlling and transforming the mind of the protagonists. The human protagonist is neither able to escape nor triumph. The Nordic landscape is since long out of human control; there remains no means to master, escape or co-exist with the local wilderness. Moreover, the anthropocentric perspective is persistently challenged by its powerful agency. Therefore, the stories constantly end in a state of uncertainty and nagging doubtfulness about human nature and its *raison d'être*. That is the true essence of horror in today's Swedish Gothic.

NOTES

An Introduction to Swedish Gothic: History and Works

1 Rosemary Jackson, *Fantasy: The Literature of Subversion*, London: Methuen, 1981, p. 173.
2 Yvonne Leffler, *I skräckens lustgård. Skräckromantik i svenska 1800-talsromaner*, diss., Göteborg: Göteborgs universitet, 1991; Yvonne Leffler 'Scandinavian Gothic', in *The Encyclopedia of the Gothic*, ed. William Hughes, David Punter and Andrew Smith, Oxford: Wiley-Blackwell, 2012, http://www.literatureencyclopedia.com; Yvonne Leffler, 'The Devious landscape of Scandinavian Horror', in *Gothic Topographies: Language, Nation Building and 'Race'*, ed. P.M. Mehtonen and M. Savolainen, Abingdon: Routledge, 2013, pp. 141–52.
3 Henrik Johnsson, *Strindberg och skräcken: skräckmotiv och identitetstematik i Strindbergs författarskap*, diss. Stockholm, Umeå: H.ström Text Kultur, 2008; Sofia Wijkmark, *Hemsökelser: Gotiken i sex berättelser av Selma Lagerlöf*, diss., Karlstad: Karlstad universitet, 2009; Mattias Fyhr, *Svensk skräcklitteratur 1: Bårtäcken över jordens likrum*, Lund: Ellerström, 2017. See also Kati Launis, 'From Italy to the Finnish Woods: The Rise of Gothic Fiction in Finland'; Pasi Nyyssönen, 'Gothic Liminality in A.H. Annilaäs Film Sauna', in *Gothic Topographies: Language: Nation Building and 'Race'*, ed. P.M. Mehtonen and Matti Savolainen, Farnham & Burlington: Ashgate, 2013, pp. 169–86, 187–202.
4 Mattias Fyhr, *De mörka labyrinterna. Gotiken i litteratur, film, musik och rollspel*, diss., Stockholm, Lund: Ellerström, 2003; Sofia Wijkmark, 'Swedish Gothic and the Demise of the Welfare State', in *Nordic Gothic*, ed. Marie Holmgren Troy, Johan Höglund, Yvonne Leffler and Sofia Wijkmark, Manchester: Manchester University Press, 2020, pp. 47–64; Yvonne Leffler, 'Nordic Gothic Crime: Places and Spaces in Johan Theorin's Öland Quartet Series', in *Nordic Gothic*, ed. Marie Holmgren Troy, Johan Höglund, Yvonne Leffler and Sofia Wijkmark, Manchester: Manchester University Press, 2020, pp. 65–83; Maria Holmgren Troy, '"The Chosen Ones": Sara B. Elfgren and Mats Stranberg's Teenage Witch Trilogy', in *Nordic Gothic*, ed. Marie Holmgren Troy, Johan Höglund, Yvonne Leffler and Sofia Wijkmark, Manchester: Manchester University Press, 2020, pp. 84–102.
5 Paula Henrikson, *Dramatikern Stagnelius*, diss. Uppsala, Stockholm and Stehag: Brutus Östlings bokförlag Symposion, 2004, p. 305.
6 Yvonne Leffler, 'From Bestselling Novelist to Forgotten Woman Writer', in *Swedish Women's Writing on Export: Tracing Transnational Reception in the Nineteenth Century*, ed. Yvonne Leffler, Åsa Arping, Jenny Bergenmar, Gunilla Hermansson and Birgitta Johansson Lindh, Göteborg: LIR.Skrifter 10, 2019, pp. 155–204.
7 Viktor Svanberg, *Rydbergs Singoalla. En studie i hans ungdomsdiktning*, diss., Uppsala, 1923, pp. 83–88.
8 Cf. Johnsson, 2008, p. 40.

9 Johnsson, 2008.

10 Göran Printz-Påhlsson, 'Krukan och bitarna', in *Perspektiv på Röda rummet. Dokument och studier samlade*, ed. Erland Lagerroth and Ulla-Britta Lagerroth, Uddevalla: Raben & Sjöberg, 1971, pp. 131–54.

11 Launis, 2013, pp. 169–86.

12 Wijkmark, 2009, pp. 169–204.

13 Wijkmark, 2009; Maria Holmgren Troy and Sofia Wijkmark, 'Two Nordic Gothic Icons: Hans Christian Andersen and Selma Lagerlöf', in *Nordic Gothic*, ed. Maria Holmgren Troy, Johan Höglund, Yvonne Leffler and Sofia Wijkmark, Manchester: Manchester University Press, 2020, pp. 29–49.

14 Sofia Wijkmark, 'Trollen i Selma Lagerlöfs "Bortbytingen" och John Ajvide Lindqvists "Gräns"', in *Spår och speglingar* [Lagerlöfstudier 2011], ed. Maria Karlsson and Louise Vinge, Möklinta: Gidlund, 2011, pp. 344–61.

15 Leffler, 1991, pp. 153–66.

16 Fred Botting, *Gothic*, 2nd ed., London and New York: Routledge, 2014, p. 150.

17 Irving Singer, *Ingmar Bergman: Cinematic Philosopher. Reflections on His Creativity*, Cambridge and London: MIT Press, 2007, p. 164.

18 John Simon, 'Conversation with Bergman', in *Ingmar Bergman: Interviews*, ed. Raphael Shargel, Durham: University Press of Mississippi, 2007, p. 75.

19 Lynda Buntzen with Carla Craig, 'Hour of the Wolf: The Case of Ingmar B.', *Film Quarterly (Archive)*; Winter 1976/1977; 30(2), p. 25.

20 José Teodoro, 'Everyone an Island: Ingmar Bergman's Second Trilogy', *Toronto International Film Festival. Archived*, 18 January 2019, https://www.tiff.net/the-review/everyone-an-island-ingmar-bergmans-second-trilogy. Retrieved 15 February 2021.

21 For an analysis of the labyrinthine structure of *Aliide, Aliide*, see Fyhr, 2003, pp. 178–203.

22 Carina Lidström, *Sökande, spegling, metamorfos. Tre vägar genom Maria Gripes skuggserie*, diss., Stockholm, Stockholm/Stehag: Symposion Graduale, 1994.

23 Maria Nilsson, *Teen Noir: Om mörkret I modern ungdomslitteratur*, Lund: BTJ förlag 2013; Yvonne Leffler, 'Female Gothic Monsters', *The History of Nordic Women's Literature*, 2016, https://nordicwomensliterature.net/2016/10/12/female-gothic-monsters/, Retrieved 3 February 2021. Troy, 2020, pp. 84–102.

24 Wijkmark, 2020, pp. 45–64. About the description of the declining folkhem in Alfredson's film based on the novel, see Helena Karlsson, 'The Vampire and the Anxieties of a Globalizing Swedish Welfare State: *Låt den rätte komma in* (*Let the Right One In*) (2008)'. *European Journal of Scandinavian Studies*, 2013; 43(2), pp. 184–99.

25 Johan Högberg, 'Nordic Gohtic New Media', in *Nordic Gothic*, ed. Maria Holmgren Troy, Johan Höglund, Yvonne Leffler and Sofia Wijkmark, Manchester: Manchester University Press, 2020, p. 171.

26 Sofia Wijkmark, 'Nordic Troll Gothic', in *Nordic Gothic*, ed. Maria Holmgren Troy, Johan Höglund, Yvonne Leffler and Sofia Wijkmark, Manchester: Manchester University Press, 2020, p. 103.

1. The Nordic Wilderness and Its Monstrous Creatures

1 Yi-Fu Tuan, *Landscapes of Fear*, Oxford: Basil Blackwell, 1980, pp. 7, 80–1 et passim. See also Yi-Fu Tuan, 'Space and Place: Humanistic Perspective', in *Philosophy in Geography*, ed. Stephen Gale and Gunnar Olsson, Dolrecht cop, 1979, pp. 387–427.

2 Yi-Fu Tuan, *Space and Place: The perspective of Experience,* London: Edward Arnold, 1977, pp. 3–18; Tuan, 1979, pp. 287–427.

3 About trolls in Nordic Gothic see Sofia Wijkmark, 'Nordic Troll Gothic', in *Nordic Gothic*, ed. Maria Holmgren Troy, Johan Höglund, Yvonne Leffler and Sofia Wijkmark, Manchester: Manchester University Press, 2020, pp. 103–124. About the film *Trollhunter* see Yvonne Leffler, 'Nordic Gothic', in *Global Gothic*, ed. Rebecca Duncan, Edinburg: Edingburg University Press, to be published in 2022/23.

4 Julia Briggs, 'The Ghost Story', in *A New Companion to the Gothic*, ed. David Punter, Chichester, UK: Wiley-Blackwell, 2012, pp. 176–85.

5 Selma Lagerlöf, *Lord Arne's Silver*, trans. Sarah Death, London: Nordic Press, 2011, p. 77.

6 Lagerlöf, 2011, p. 23.

7 Lagerlöf, 2011, p. 28.

8 William Patrick Day, *In the Circles of Fear and Desire: A Study of Gothic Fantasy*, Chicago and London: The University of Chicago Press, 1985, p. 6.

9 Kate Ferguson Ellis, *The Contested Castle: Gothic Novels and the Subversion of Domestic Ideology*, Urbana: University of Illinois Press, 1989, p. 166.

10 Henrik, Johnsson, 'Archipelago', in *Nordic Literature: A Comparative History. Volume I: Spatial Nodes*, ed. Steven P. Sondrup, Mark B Sandberg, Thomas A. DuBois and Dan Ringgaard, Amsterdam/Philadelphia: John Benjamins Publishing Company, 2017, p. 169.

11 Sofia Wijkmark, *Hemsökelser. Gotiken i sex berättelser av Selma Lagerlöf*, diss., Karlstad: Karlstad University Studies 20, 2009, pp. 205–23.

12 Wijkmark, 2020, pp. 113–21; Adriana Margareta Dancus, 'Trollism, Reality Hunger, and Vulnerability. Trolls in Film and Literature in the 2000's', *De Gruyter*, 2016; 46(2), pp. 256–58, 260.

13 Stefan Spjut, *Stallo* (2012), Stockholm: Albert Bonniers förlag, 2013, p. 73, 342.

14 John Ajvide Lindqvist, 'Gräns', in *Pappersväggar. Tio berättelser*, Stockholm: Ordfront, 2007, p. 30.

15 Sofia Wijkmark, 'Trollen i Selma Lagerlöfs 'Bortbytingen'', in *Spår och speglingar. Lagerlöfstudier 2011*, ed. Maria Karlsson and Louise Vinge, Möklinta: Gidlunds förlag, 2011, och John Afvide Lindqvist, 2007, pp. 356–57.

16 Interview by Cajsa Collin, 'Sweden's Debate: How Warmly to Welcome Outsiders', *US News and World Report*, 10 July 2017. https://www.usnews.com/news/best-countris/articles/2027-07-10/immigration-forces-sweden-to-re-evaluate-its-welfare-state, Retrieved 20 October 2021.

17 Rebecca Pulsifer, 'Trolling Humanism: New Materialist Performativity in Border', *Gender Forum: And Internet Journal for Gender Studies*, 2019; 17, p. 19.

18 Timothy Morton, *The Ecological Thought*, Cambridge, MA, and London: Harvard University Press, 2010, p. 7.

19 About EcoGothic in American and Canadian literature, see Andrew Smith and William Hughes (eds.), *Ecogothic*, Manchester: Manchester University Press, 2013.

20 Dancus, 2016, pp. 253, 265–6.

2. The Gender-Coded Landscape and Transgressive Female Monsters

1 Anne Williams, *Art of Darkness: A Poetics of Gothic*, Chicago and London: Chicago University Press, 1995.

2 Kate Ferguson Ellis, *The Contested Castle: Gothic Novels and the Subversion of Domestic Ideology*, Urbana and Chicago: University of Illinois Press, 1989.

3 Diana Wallace and Andrew Smith, 'Introduction: Defining the Female Gothic', in *The Female Gothic: New Directions*, ed. Diana Wallace and Andrew Smith, Palgrave Macmillan UK, 2009. ProQuest Ebook Central, Http://ebookcetral.proqust.com/lib/gu/detail.action?docI(D=578852, p. 3.

4 Elizabeth Parker, *The Forest and the EcoGothic: The Deep Dark Woods in the Popular Imagination*, [Palgrave Gothic] London: Palgrave Macmillan, 2020, pp. 28, 113–31.

5 Viktor Svanberg, *Rydbergs Singoalla. En studie i hans ungdomsdiktning*, diss., Uppsala 1923, pp. 83–8.

6 Yvonne Leffler, *I skräckens lustgård. Skräckromantik i svenska 1800-talsromaner*, diss., Göteborg: Göteborgs universitet, 1991, pp. 121–52.

7 Glennis Byron, 'Gothic in the 1890's', in *A New Companion to the Gothic*, ed. David Punter, Chichester: Wiley-Blackwell, 2012, p. 193.

8 Fred Botting, *Gothic: The New Critical Idiom*, 2nd ed., New York: Routledge, 2014, pp. 84–5.

9 See anonymous review on *Culture Crypt* https://culturecrypt.com/movie-reviews/wither-2012. Retrieved 18 February 2021; Mats Johnson, *Göteborgs-Posten*, 9 August 2013, https://www.gp.se/kultur/film-tv/vittra-1.571650. Retrieved 9 November 2021.

10 Brandyn Whitaker, *The Forest Is Not What It Seems: An Ecocritical Study of American Horror Films*, Master thesis, Middle Tennessee State University, 2020, pp. 73–111.

11 The stories and their characters re-appear in Anders Fager's role-play *Svenska kulter* (2014).

12 H.P. Lovecraft, *Supernatural Horror in Literature*. With a New Introduction by E.F. Bleiler, New York: Dover Publication, 1973, p. 15.

13 Juliann E. Fleenor, 'Introduction: The Female Gothic', in *The Female Gothic*, ed. Juliann E. Fleenor, Montréal and London: Eden Press, 1983, p. 11.

14 Fleenor, 1983, p. 11.

15 Maria Holmgren Troy, '"The Chosen Ones": Sara B. Elfgren and Mats Sandberg's Teenage Witch Trilogy', in *Nordic Gothic*, ed. Maria Holmgren Troy, Johan Höglund, Yvonne Leffler, and Sofia Wijkmark, Manchester: Manchester University Press, 2020, s. 84–7.

16 William Patrick Day, *In the Circles of Fear and Desire: A Study of Gothic Fantasy*, Chicago and London: The University of Chicago Press,1985, pp. 5, 75–8.

17 Day, 1985, pp. 17–27, 76, 151, 157 et passim.

18 Ellen Moer, *Literary Women* (1963). With a new introduction by Helen Taylor, London: The Women's Press, 1986, p. 127.

19 Day, 1985, pp. 103–5.

20 *Ecofeminism*. https://en.wikipedia.org/wiki/Ecofeminism, Retrieved 15 June 2021.

3. Nordic Noir and Gothic Crimes

1 William Patrick Day, *In the Circles of Fear and Desire: A Study of Gothic Fantasy*, Chicago and London: The University of Chicago Press, 1985, pp. 4–5, 50–9; Maurizio Ascari and Stephen Knight (eds.), *From the Sublime to City Crime*, Monaco: Liber Faber, 2015.

2 Yvonne Leffler, 'Early Crime Fiction in Nordic Literature', in *From the Sublime to City Crime*, ed. Maurizio Ascari and Stephen Knight, Monaco: Liber Faber, 2015, pp. 161–82.

3 Yvonne Leffler, 'Nordic Gothic Crime: Place and Spaces in Johan Theorin's Öland Quartet Series', in *Nordic Gothic*, ed. Maria Holmgren Troy, Johan Höglund, Yvonne Leffler and Sofia Wijkmark, Manchester: Manchester University Press, 2020, pp. 65–83.

4 The role of the forest in *Twin Peaks* has been studied by Elisabeth Parker in Parker, *The Forest and the EcoGothic: The Deep Dark Woods in the Popular Imagination*, [Palgrave Gothic] London: Palgrave Macmillan, 2020, pp. 94–100.

5 James Donaghy, 'Murder, Mystery, Evil Swedish Forests: Have You Been Watching Jordskott?', *The Guardian*, 14 July 2015.

6 In Swedish: 'hade blivit ovän med skogen' (part 2); 'den naturen tar, släpper den inte' (part 5).

7 In Swedish 'behöver det'.

8 Stacy Alaimo, *Bodily Natures: Science, Environment, and the Material Self*, Bloomington: Indiana University press, 2010, p. 4.

9 Irina Souch, 'Transformations of the Evil Forest in the Swedish Television Series *Jordskott*: An Ecocritical Reading', *Nordicom Review*, 2020; 4 (Special Issues), p. 111, 117 et passim. https://doi.org/10.2478/nor-2020-0011. Retrieved 11 November 2021.

10 Cecilia Ekbäck, *In the Month of the Midnight Sun*, London Hodder & Stoughton, 2016, p. 33.

11 Ekbäck, 2016, p. 56.

12 Ekbäck, 2016, p. 186.

13 Ekbäck, 2016, p. 120.

14 Judith Halberstam, *Skin Shows: Gothic Horror and the Technology of Monsters*, Durham and London: Duke University Press: 1995, p. 19, cf. also pp. 1–11, 178 et passim. Cf. Sigmund Freud and Josef Breuer, *Studies on Hysteria* (1893), trans. and ed. James and Alix Strachery [The Pelican Freud Library volume 3], New York: Penguin Books, 1980, pp. 56–7.

15 Ekbäck, 2016, p. 115.

16 David Punter, *The Literature of Terror: A History of Gothic Fictions from 1765 to the Present Day* (1978). Volume II: The Modern Gothic, 2nd ed., London and New York: Longman 1996, p. 183.

17 Fred Botting, 'In Gothic Darkly: Heterotopia, History, Culture', in *A New Companion to the Gothic*, ed. David Punter, Chichester, UK: Wiley-Blackwell, 2012, p. 19, 13–24. Michel Foucault, 'Of Other Spaces', *Diacrtics*, 1986; 16(1), p. 24.

18 Rebecca Duncan, *South African Gothic: Anxiety and Creative Dissent in the Post-apartheid Imagination and Beyond*, Cardiff: University of Wales Press, 2018, p. 41, 193 et passim.

LIST OF SWEDISH TITLES REFERRED TO IN THE BOOK

Sorted on author/director and Swedish source title with its published English title(s) within parenthesis. If it is not published in English, a literary translation of the Swedish title is given within parenthesis but without year of publication.

Literary Works

Almqvist, Carl Jonas Love, *Amorina*, 1821 (Amorina)
    Palatset, 1838 (The Palace)
    Skällnora qvarn, 1838 (Skällnora Mill)
Axelsson, Majgull, *Aprilhäxan*, 1997 (April Witch, 2002)
Bäck, Madeleine, *Berget offrar*, 2018 (The Mountain Sacrifices)
    Jorden vaknar, 2017 (The Soil Arouses)
    Vattnet drar, 2015 (The Water Draws)
Ekbäck, Cecilia, *Midnattssolens timme*, 2016 (In the Month of the Midnight Sun, 2016)
    I vargavinterns land, 2015 (Wolf Winter, 2015)
Ekman, Kerstin, *Händelser vid vatten*, 1993 (Blackwater, 1995)
Fager, Anders, *Samlade svenska kulter*, 2011 (Collected Swedish Cults)
Flygare-Carlén, Emilie, *Rosen på Tistelön*, 1842 (The Rose of Tistelön, 1844; The Rose of Thistle Isle, 1844; The Smugglers of the Swedish Coast, or, The Rose of Thistle Island, 1844)
Gripe, Maria *Skuggserien*, 1982–88 (The Shadow Series)
Hagberg, Matthias, *Rekviem för en vanskapt*, 2012 (Requiem for a Disable)
Ingelius, Axel Gabriel, *Det gråa slottet*, 1851 (The Grey Castle)
Jensen, Caroline L. *Vargsläkte*, 2011 (Wolf Kindred)
Kandre, Mare, *Aliide, Aliide*, 1991 (Aliide, Aliide)
    Bestiarium, 1999 (Bestiarium)
    Bübins unge, 1987 (Bübin's Offspring)
Lagerlöf, Selma, 'Bortbytingen', 1915 (The Changeling)
    En herrgårdssägen, 1899 (From a Swedish Homestead, 1901; The Tale of a Manor, 1922; A Manor House Tale, 2015)
    'Frid på jorden' (Peace on Earth)
    Gösta Berlings Saga, 1891 (The Story of Gösta Berling, 1898; *Gösta Berling's Saga*, 1918)

Herr Arnes penningar, 1903 (Herr Arne's Hoard, 1923; The Treasure, 1925; Lord Arne's Silver, 2011)

'Karln', 1891 (The Bloke)

Körkarlen, 1912 (The Soul Shall Bear Witness, 1921; The Phantom Carriage, 2011)

'Stenkumlet' (The King's Grave)

'Spökhanden', 1898 (The Ghost's Hand)

Troll och människor, 1915 (Troll and Humans)

Lagerkvist, Pär, 'Far och jag', 1924 (Father and I)

Onda sagor, 1924 (Evil Tales)

Linder, Marie, *En qvinna af vår tid*, 1867 (A Woman of Our Time)

Linderholm, Helmer, *De ulvgrå*, 1972 (The Wolfish Grey)

Lindqvist, John Ajvide, *Gräns*, 2006 (Border)

Hanteringen av odöda, 2005 (Handling the Undead, 2008)

Låt den rätte komma in, 2004 (Let the Right One In, 2007; Let Me In, 2007)

Människohamn, 2008 (Harbour, 2010)

Livijn, Clas, 'Samvetets fantasi', 1821 (A Fantasy of the Conscience)

Ljungstedt, Aurora, *Hin Ondes hus*, 1853 (The House of the Devil)

Ohlmarks, Åke, *Gengångare*, 1971 (Revenants)

Slottsspöken, 1973 (Castle Ghosts)

Rydberg, Viktor, *Singoalla*, 1857 (Singoalla, 1903)

Vampyren, 1848 (The Vampire)

Spjut, Stefan, *Stallo*, 2012 (The Shapeshifter, 2015; Stallo, 2015)

Stalpi, 2017 (Trolls, 2019; Stalpi)

Stagnelius, Erik Johan, *Albert och Julia*, 1825 (Albert and Julia)

Glädjeflickan i Rom, 1825 (The Prostitute in Rome)

Riddartornet, 1821–23 (The Knight's Tower)

Strandberg, Mats, *Färjan*, 2015 (Blood Cruise, 2018)

Hemmet, 2017 (The Home, 2020)

Strandberg, Mats, and Sara B. Elfgren, *Cirkeln*, 2011 (The Circle, 2012)

Eld, 2012 (Fire, 2012)

Nyckeln, 2013 (The Key, 2015)

Strindberg, August, *Röda rummet*, 1879 (The Red Room, 1913)

Spöksonaten, 1907 (Ghost Sonata, 1976)

Tschandala, 1888 (Tschandala, 2007)

Theorin, Johan, *Blodläge*, 2010 (The Quarry, 2011)

Nattfåk, 2008 (The Darkest Room, 2009)

Rörgast, 2013 (The Voices Beyond, 2016)

Skumtimmen, 2007 (Echoes from the Dead, 2009)

Topelius, Zacharias, *En natt och en morgon*, 1843 (A Night and a Morning)

Gröna kammarn i Linnais gård, 1859 (The Green Chamber at Linnais Mansion)

Trotzig, Birgitta, *Dykungens dotter*, 1985 (The Mud-King's Daughter)

Films and TV Drama

Abassi, Ali, *Gräns*, Sweden, 2018 (Border)

Alfredson, Tomas, *Låt den rätte komma in*, Sweden, 2008 (Let the Right One In)

Banke, Anders, *Frostbiten*, Sweden, 2006 (Frostbitten; Frostbite)

Bergman, Ingmar, *Det sjunde inseglet*, Sweden, 1957 (The Seventh Seal)

Persona, Sweden, 1966 (Persona)

Vargtimmen, Sweden, 1968 (Hour of the Wolf)

Björn, Henrik *Jordskott*, Season 1, Swedish Televison, 2015 (Soil Sprouts)

Blomberg, Erik, *Valkoinen peura/Den vita renen*, Sweden, 1952 (The White Reindeer)

Christensen, Benjamin, *Häxan*, Denmark & Sweden, 1922 (The Witches, Am. Title: Witchcraft Through the Ages)

Conell, Jonas, *Månguden*, Swedish Television, 1988 (The Moon God)

Ersgård, Joakim, *Besökarna*, Sweden, 1988 (The Visitors)

Hatwig, Hans, *Blödaren*, Sweden, 1983 (The Bleeder)

Hjorth, Michael, *Det okända*, Sweden, 2000 (The Unknown)

Jacobsson, Anders, *Evil Ed*, Sweden, 1995 (Evil Ed)

Krantz, Leif, *Kråkguldet*, Swedish Television, 1969 (Crows' Gold)

Kullamannen, Swedish Television, 1967 (The Kullen Man)

Laguna, Sonny and Tommy Wiklund, *Vittra*, Sweden, 2012 (Wither)

Mårlind, Måns and Björn Stein, *Midnattsol/Jour polaire*, Sweden, France, 2016 (Midnight Sun)

Sjöström, Victor, *Körkarlen*, Sweden, 1921 (The Phantom Carriage)

Tivemark, Thomas, *Ängelby*, Swedish Television, 2015 (Ängelby)

Vogel, Virgil W., *Rymdinvation i Lappland*, Sweden, USA, 1959 (Terror in the Midnight Sun)

BIBLIOGRAPHY

Alaimo, Stacy, *Bodily Natures: Science, Environment, and the Material Self*, Bloomington: Indiana University Press, 2010.

Anon., *Ecofeminism*. https://en..wikipedia.org./wiki/Ecofeminism (retrieved 15 June 2021).

Anon., *Review on Culture Crypt*. https://culturecrypt.com/movie-reviews/wither-2012 (retrieved 18 February 2021).

Ascari, Maurizio and Stephen Knight (eds.), *From the Sublime to City Crime*, Monaco: Liber Faber, 2015.

Botting, Fred, *Gothic*, 2nd ed, London and New York: Routledge, 2014.

Botting, Fred, 'In Gothic Darkly: Heterotopia, History, Culture', in David Punter (ed.), *A New Companion to the Gothic*, Chichester, UK: Wiley-Blackwell, 2012, pp. 13–24.

Briggs, Julia, 'The Ghost Story', in David Punter (ed.), *A New Companion to the Gothic*, Chichester, UK: Wiley-Blackwell, 2012, pp. 176–85.

Buntzen, Lynda with Carla Craig, 'Hour of the Wolf: The Case of Ingmar B.', *Film Quarterly (Archive)*; Winter 1976/1977; 30(2), pp. 23–34.

Byron, Glennis, 'Gothic in the 1890's', in David Punter (ed.), *A New Companion to the Gothic*, Chichester: Wiley-Blackwell, 2012, pp. 186–96.

Collin, Cajsa, 'Sweden's Debate: How Warmly to Welcome Outsiders,' *US News and World Report*, 10 July 2017. https://www.usnews.com/news/best-countris/articles/2027-07 -10/immigration-forces-sweden-to-re-evaluate-its-welfare-state (retrieved 10 October 2021).

Dancus, Adriana Margareta, 'Trollism, Reality Hunger, and Vulnerability. Trolls in film and literature in the 2000's', *De Gruyter*, 2016; 46(2), pp. 250–69.

Day, William Patrick, *In the Circles of Fear and Desire: A Study of Gothic Fantasy*, Chicago and London: The University of Chicago Press, 1985.

Donaghy, James, 'Murder, Mystery, Evil Swedish Forests: Have You Been Watching Jordskott?', *The Guardian*, 14 July 2015.

Duncan, Rebecca, *South African Gothic: Anxiety and Creative Dissent in the Post-apartheid Imagination and Beyond*, Cardiff: University of Wales Press, 2018.

Ekbäck, Cecilia, *In the Month of the Midnight Sun*, London: Hodder & Stoughton, 2016.

Ellis, Kate Ferguson, *The Contested Castle: Gothic Novels and the Subversion of Domestic Ideology*, Urbana: University of Illinois Press, 1989.

Fleenor, Juliann E., 'Introduction: The Female Gothic', in Juliann E. Fleenor (ed.), *The Female Gothic*, Montréal and London: Eden Press, 1983.

Foucault, Michael, 'Of Other Spaces', *Diacrtics*, 1986; 16(1), pp. 22–27.

Freud, Sigmund and Josef Breuer, *Studies on Hysteria* (1893), trans. and ed. James and Alix Strachery [The Pelican Freud Library volume 3], New York: Penguin Books, 1980.

Fyhr, Mattias, *De mörka labyrinterna. Gotiken i litteratur, film, musik och rollspel*, diss., Stockholm, Lund: Ellerström, 2003.

Fyhr, Mattias, *Svensk skräcklitteratur 1: Bårtäcken över jordens likrum*, Lund: Ellerström, 2017.

Halberstam, Judith, *Skin Shows: Gothic Horror and the Technology of Monsters*, Durham and London: Duke University Press: 1995,

Henrikson, Paula, *Dramatikern Stagnelius*, diss. Uppsala, Stockholm and Stehag: Brutus Östlings bokförlag Symposion, 2004.

Högberg, Johan, 'Nordic Gothic New Media', in Maria Holmgren Troy, Johan Höglund, Yvonne Leffler, and Sofia Wijkmark (eds.), *Nordic Gothic*, Manchester: Manchester University press, 2020, pp. 169–90.

Jackson, Rosemay, *Fantasy: The Literature of Subversion*, London: Methuen, 1981.

Johnson, Mats, *Göteborgs Posten*, 9 August 2013, https://www.gp.se/kultur/film-tv/vittra-1.571650 (retrieved 9 November 2021).

Johnsson, Henrik, 'Archipelago', in Steven P. Sondrup, Mark B Sandberg, Thomas A. DuBois and Dan Ringgaard (eds.), *Nordic Literature: A Comparative History. Volume I: Spatial Nodes*, Amsterdam/Philadelphia: John Benjamins Publishing Company, 2017, pp. 162–72.

Johnsson, Henrik, *Strindberg och skräcken: skräckmotiv och identitetstematik i Strindbergs författarskap*, diss. Stockholm, Umeå: H.ström Text Kultur, 2008.

Karlsson, Helena, 'The Vampire and the Anxieties of a Globalizing Swedish Welfare State: Låt den rätte komma in (Let the Right One In) (2008)', *European Journal of Scandinavian Studies*, 2013; 43(2), pp. 184–99.

Lagerlöf, Selma, *Lord Arne's Silver*, trans. Sarah Death, London: Nordic Press, 2011.

Launis, Kati, 'From Italy to the Finnish Woods: The Rise of Gothic Fiction in Finland' in P.M. Mehtonen and Matti Savolainen (eds.), *Gothic Topographies: Language: Nation Building and 'Race'*, Farnham & Burlington: Ashgate, 2013, pp. 169–86.

Leffler, Yvonne, 'Early Crime Fiction in Nordic Literature', in Maurizio Ascari and Stephen Knight (eds.), *From the Sublime to City Crime*, Monaco: Liber Faber, 2015, pp. 161–82.

Leffler, Yvonne, 'Female Gothic Monsters', *The History of Nordic Women's Literature*, 2016, https://nordicwomensliterature.net/2016/10/12/female-gothic-monsters/ (retrieved 3 February 2021).

Leffler, Yvonne, 'From Bestselling Novelist to Forgotten Woman Writer', in Yvonne Leffler, Åsa Arping, Jenny Bergenmar, Gunilla Hermansson and Birgitta Johansson Lindh (eds.), *Swedish Women's Writing on Export: Tracing Transnational Reception in the Nineteenth Century*, Göteborg: LIR.Skrifter 10, 2019, pp. 155–204.

Leffler, Yvonne, *I skräckens lustgård. Skräckromantik i svenska 1800-talsromaner.* Diss., Göteborg: Göteborgs universitet, 1991.

Leffler, Yvonne, 'Nordic Gothic', in Rebecca Duncan, *Global Gothic*, Edinburgh: Edinburgh University Press, to be published in 2022/2023.

Leffler, Yvonne, 'Nordic Gothic Crime: Places and Spaces in Johan Theorin's Öland Quartet Series', in Marie Holmgren Troy, Johan Höglund, Yvonne Leffler and Sofia Wijkmark (eds.), *Nordic Gothic*, Manchester: Manchester University Press, 2020, pp. 65–83.

Leffler, Yvonne, 'Scandinavian Gothic', in William Hughes, David Punter and Andrew Smith (eds.), *The Encyclopedia of the Gothic*, Oxford: Wiley-Blackwell, 2012, http://www.literatureencyclopedia.com

Leffler, Yvonne, 'The Devious landscape of Scandinavian Horror', in P.M. Mehtonen and M. Savolainen (eds.), *Gothic Topographies: Language, Nation Building and 'Race'*, Abingdon: Routledge, 2013, pp. 141–52.

Lidström, Carina, *Sökande, spegling, metamorfos. Tre vägar genom Maria Gripes skuggserie*, diss., Stockholm, Stockholm/Stehag: Symposion Graduale, 1994.

Lindqvist, John Ajvide, 'Gräns', in *Pappersväggar. Tio berättelser*, Stockholm: Ordfront, 2007, pp. 9–73.

Lovecraft, H.P., *Supernatural Horror in Literature*. With a New Introduction by E.F. Bleiler, New York: Dover Publication, 1973.

Moer, Ellen, *Literary Women* (1963). With a new introduction by Helen Taylor, London: The Women's Press, 1986.

Morton, Timothy, *The Ecological Thought*, Cambridge, MA, and London: Harvard University Press, 2010.

Nilson, Maria, *Teen Noir: Om mörkret i modern ungdomslitteratur*, Lund: BTJ förlag 2013.

Nyyssönen, Pasi, 'Gothic Liminality in A.H. Annilaäs Film Sauna', in P.M. Mehtonen and Matti Savolainen (eds.), *Gothic Topographies: Language: Nation Building and 'Race'*, Farnham & Burlington: Ashgate, 2013, pp. 187–202.

Parker, Elizabeth, *The Forest and the EcoGothic: The Deep Dark Woods in the Popular Imagination*, [Palgrave Gothic] London: Palgrave Macmillan, 2020.

Printz-Påhlsson, Göran, 'Krukan och bitarna', in Erland Lagerroth and Ulla-Britta Lagerroth (eds.), *Perspektiv på Röda rummet. Dokument och studier samlade*, Uddevalla: Raben & Sjöberg, 1971, pp. 131–54.

Pulsifer, Rebecca, 'Trolling Humanism: New Materialist Performativity in Border', *Gender Forum: And Internet Journal for Gender Studies*, 2019; 17, pp. 7–22.

Punter, David, *The Literature of Terror: A History of Gothic Fictions from 1765 to the Present Day (1978). Volume II: The Modern Gothic*, 2nd ed., London and New York: Longman, 1996.

Simon, John, 'Conversation with Bergman', in Raphael Shargel (ed.), *Ingmar Bergman: Interviews*, Durham: University Press of Mississippi, 2007, pp. 69–95.

Singer, Irving, *Ingmar Bergman, Cinematic Philosopher. Reflections on His Creativity*, Cambridge and London: MIT Press, 2007.

Smith, Andrew, and William Hughes (eds.), *Ecogothic*, Manchester: Manchester University Press, 2013.

Smith, Diana Andrew (eds.), *The Female Gothic: New Directions*, Palgrave Macmillan UK, 2009. ProQuest Ebook Central, Http://ebookcetral.proqust.com/lib/gu/detail.action?docI(D=578852

Souch, Irina, 'Transformations of the Evil Forest in the Swedish Television Series *Jordskott*: An Ecocritical reading', *Nordicom Review*, 2020; 4(Special Issues), pp. 107–22, doi: 10.2478/nor-2020-0011 (retrieved 11 November 2021).

Spjut, Stefan, *Stallo (2012)*, Stockholm: Albert Bonniers förlag, 2013.

Svanberg, Viktor, *Rydbergs Singoalla. En studie i hans ungdomsdiktning*, diss., Uppsala, 1923.

Teodoro, José, 'Everyone an Island: Ingmar Bergman's Second Trilogy', *Toronto International Film Festival. Archived*, 18 January 2019, https://www.tiff.net/the-review/everyone-an-island-ingmar-bergmans-second-trilogy (retrieved 15 February 2021).

Troy, Maria Holmgren, 'The Chosen Ones': Sara B. Elfgren and Mats Stranberg's teenage witch trilogy', in Marie Holmgren Troy, Johan Höglund, Yvonne Leffler and Sofia Wijkmark (eds.), *Nordic Gothic*, Manchester: Manchester University Press, 2020, pp. 84–102.

Troy, Maria Holmgren and Sofia Wijkmark, 'Two Nordic Gothic Icons: Hans Christian Andersen and Selma Lagerlöf', in Maria Holmgren Troy, Johan Höglund, Yvonne Leffler and Sofia Wijkmark (eds.), *Nordic Gothic*, Manchester: Manchester University Press, 2020, pp. 29–49.

Tuan, Yi-Fu, *Landscapes of Fear*, Oxford: Basil Blackwell, 1980.

Tuan, Yi-Fu, 'Space and Place: Humanistic Perspective', in Stephen Gale and Gunnar Olsson (eds.), *Philosophy in Geography*, Dolrecht cop, 1979, pp. 387–427.

Tuan, Yi-Fu *Space and Place: The perspective of Experience*, London: Edward Arnold, 1977.

Whitaker, Brandyn, *The Forest Is Not What It Seems: An Ecocritical Study of American Horror Films*, Master thesis, ProQuest dissertation, Middle Tennessee State University, 2020.

Wijkmark, Sofia, *Hemsökelser: Gotiken i sex berättelser av Selma Lagerlöf*, diss., Karlstad: Karlstad universitet, 2009.

Wijkmark, Sofia, 'Nordic troll Gothic', in Maria Holmgren Troy, Johan Höglund, Yvonne Leffler, and Sofia Wijkmark (eds.), *Nordic Gothic*, Manchester: Manchester University press, 2020, pp. 103–24.

Wijkmark, Sofia, 'Swedish Gothic and the Demise of the Welfare State', in Marie Holmgren Troy, Johan Höglund, Yvonne Leffler and Sofia Wijkmark (eds.), *Nordic Gothic*, Manchester: Manchester University Press, 2020, pp. 47–64.

Wijkmark, Sofia, 'Trollen i Selma Lagerlöfs "Bortbytingen" och John Ajvide Lindqvists "Gräns"', in Maria Karlsson and Louise Vinge (eds.), *Spår och speglingar* [Lagerlöfstudier 2011], Möklinta: Gidlund, 2011, pp. 344–61.

Williams, Anne, *Art of Darkness: A Poetics of Gothic*, Chicago and London: Chicago University Press, 1995.

INDEX

Abassi, Ali 18
Alaimo, Stacy 54
Albert and Julia (Stagnelius) 2
Alfredson, Tomas 14
Aliide, Aliide (Kandre) 12
Almqvist, Carl Jonas Love 3
The Amityville Horror (Rosenberg) 11
Amorina, (Almqvist) 3
Andersen, H. C. 12
Ängelby (Tivemark) 15
April Witch (Axelsson) 12
Ascari, Maurizio 70
Axelsson, Majgull 12

Bäck, Madeleine 14
Banke, Anders 13
Bergman, Ingmar 9
Bestiarium (Kandre) 12
Björn, Henrik 15
Blackwater (Ekman) 11
The Blair Witch Project (Myrick, Sánchez) 13
The Bleeder (Hatwig) 11
'The Bloke' (Lagerlöf) 8
Blomberg, Erik 10
Blood Cruise (Strandberg) 13
Border (Abassi) 18
Border (Lindqvist) 14
Botting, Fred 9
Breuer, Josef 71
The Bridge (Rosenfelt) 49
Briggs, Julia 19
Bübin's Offspring (Kandre) 12
Buntzen; Lynda 10
Byron, Glennis 37

Castle Ghosts (Ohlmarks) 13
Celina, or the Mystery Child (Ducray-Duminil) 2
'The Changeling' (Lagerlöf) 8
Christensen, Benjamin 9
The Circle (Strandberg, Elfgren) 14
Collected Swedish Cults (Fager) 13

Collin, Cajsa 69
Cooper, Marian C. 11
Crows' Gold (Krantz) 12

Dahl, Gunnar 12
Dancus, Adriana Margareta 25
Danielsson, Dagmar 12–13
The Darkest Room (Theorin) 15Day, William Patrick 22
'The Dead Woman in Love' (Gautier) 6
Disney, Walt 9
Donaghy, James 52
Dracula (Stoker) 7
Ducray-Duminil, François Guillaume 2
Duncan, Rebecca 62

Echoes from the Dead (Theorin) 15
Ekbäck, Cecilia 15
Ekman, Kerstin 11
Eleonora Rosalba (Radcliffe) 2
Elfgren, Sara B. 14
Ellis, Kate Ferguson 23
Ersgård, Joakim 11
The Evil Dead (Raimi) 13
Evil Ed (Jacobsson) 13
Evil Tales (Lagerkvist) 9

Fager, Anders 13
'The Fall of the House of Usher' (Poe) 4
Fantasia (Disney) 9
'A Fantasy of the Conscience'(Livijn) 3
'Father and I' (Lagerkvist) 9
Fire (Strandberg, Elfgren) 14
Fleenor, Juliann E. 42
Flygare-Carlén, Emilie 5
Foucault, Michael 61
Freud, Sigmund 25
*Friday the 13*th (Cunningham) 11
Frostbite (Banke) 13
Fyhr, Mattias 1

Gautier, Théophile 6
Ghost Sonata (Strindberg) 7

'The Ghost's Hand' (Lagerlöf) 8
The Ghost-Seer (Schiller) 2
Goethe, Johann Wolfgang 2
The Golden Pot (Hoffmann) 10
Gösta Berling's Saga (Lagerlöf) 8
Götz von Berlichingen (Goethe) 2
The Green Chamber at Linnais Mansion
    (Topelius) 6
The Grey Castle (Ingelius) 6
Grimm, Brothers 12
Gripe, Maria 12

Hagberg, Matthias 15
Halberstam, Judith 59
Handling the Undead (Lindqvist) 14
Harbour (Lindqvist) 14
Hatwig, Hans 11
Henrikson, Paula 67
Hjorth, Michael 13
Hoffmann, E.T.A. 2
Högberg, Johan 15
The Home (Strandberg) 14
Hour of the Wolf (Bergman) 10
The House of the Devil (Ljungstedt) 6

In the Month of the Midnight Sun (Ekbäck) 11
Ingelius, Axel Gabriel 6
The Italian (Radcliffe) 2

Jackson, Rosemay 1
Jacobsson, Anders 13
Jensen, Caroline L. 14
Johnson, Mats 70
Johnsson, Henrik 1

Kandre, Mare 12
Karlsson, Helena 68
The Key (Strandberg, Elfgren) 14
The Killing (Sveistrup) 49
King Kong (Cooper, Schoedsack) 11
'The King's Grave' (Lagerlöf) 8
Knight, Stephen 70
The Knight's Tower (Stagnelius) 2
Krantz, Leif 12
Kubrick, Stanley 10
The Kullen Man (Krantz) 12

Lagerkvist, Pär 9
Lagerlöf, Selma 1
Laguna, Sonny 13
Larsson, Stieg 49
Launis, Kati 8
Leffler, Yvonne 1

Let Me In (Reeves) 14
Let the Right One in (Alfredson) 14
Let the Right One in (Lindqvist) 14
Lewis, Matthew 2
Lidström, Carina 12
Linder, Marie 8
Linderholm, Helmer 13
Lindqvist, John Ajvide 14
Livijn, Clas 3f
Ljungstedt, Aurora 6
Lord Arne's Silver (Lagerlöf) 8
Lovecraft, H.P. 40

'The Magnetiser' (Hoffmann) 2
Mankell, Henning 49
A Manor House Tale (Lagerlöf) 8
Mårlind, Måns 15
Matheson, Richard 12
Midnight Sun (Mårlind, Stein) 15
Moer, Ellen 48
The Monk (Lewis) 2
The Moon God (Conell) 11
Morton, Timothy 32
The Mountain Sacrifices (Bäck) 14
The Mud-king's Daughter (Trotzig) 12
Mussorgsky, Modest 9
Myrick, Daniel 13
The Mystery of Udolpho (Radcliffe) 2

'A Night and a Morning' (Topelius) 4–5
Night on Bald Mountain (Mussorgsky) 9
Nyyssönen, Pasi 67

Ohlmarks, Åke 13

The Palace (Alqmvist) 4
Parker, Elizabeth 35
'Peace on Earth' (Lagerlöf) 8
Persona (Bergman) 10
The Phantom Carriage (Lagerlöf) 9
The Phantom Carriage (Sjöström) 9
Poe, Edgar Allan 4
Polidori, John 6
Printz-Påhlsson, Göran 68
The Prostitute in Rome (Stagnelius) 2
Pulsifer, Rebecca 31
Punter, David 60

The Quarry (Theorin) 15

Radcliffe, Ann 2
Raimi, Sam 13
The Red Room (Strindberg) 7

Reeves, Matt 14
Requiem for a Disable (Hagberg) 15
Revenants (Ohlmarks) 13
The Robbers (Schiller) 2
The Rose of Tistelön (Flygare-Carlén) 5
Rosenberg, Stuart) 11
Rydberg, Viktor 6

Sánchez, Eduardo 13
Schiller, Friedrich 2
Schoedsack, Ernest 11
The Seventh Seal (Bergman) 9
The Shadow Series (Gripe) 12
The Shining (Kubrick) 10
Simon, John 68
Singer, Irving 10
Singoalla (Rydberg) 6
Sjöström, Victor 9
Skällnora Mill (Almqvist) 4
Smith, Andrew 35
The Soil Arouses (Bäck) 14
Soil Sprouts (Björn) 15
Souch, Irina 54
Spjut, Stefan 15
Stagnelius, Erik Johan 2
Stallo (Spjut) 15
Stalpi (Spjut) 15
Stein, Björn 15
Stevenson, Robert Louis 7
Stoker, Bram 7
Strandberg, Mats 14
The Strange Case of Dr Jekyll and Mr Hyde
    (Stevenson) 7
Strindberg, August 1
Svanberg, Viktor 6

Teodoro, José 10

Terror in the Midnight Sun (Vogel) 11
Theorin, Johan 15
Tivemark, Thomas 15
Topelius, Zacharias 4
Troll and Humans (Lagerlöf) 18
Trotzig, Birgitta 12
Troy, Maria Holmgren 46
Tschandala (Strindberg) 7
Tuan, Yi-Fu 17
The Tunnel (MacDonald) 49

'The Uncanny Guest'(Hoffmann) 2
The Unknown (Hjort) 13

The Vampire (Polidori) 6
The Vampire (Rydberg) 6
Viktor, a Child of the Forest (Ducray-
    Duminil) 2
The Visitors (Ersgård) 11
Vogel, Virgil W. 11
The Voices Beyond (Theorin) 15

The Water Draws (Bäck) 14
Whitaker, Brandyn 70
The White Reindeer (Blomberg) 10–11
Wijkmark, Sofia 1
Wiklund, Tommy 13
Williams, Anne 35
The Witches (Christensen) 9
Wither (Laguna, Wiklund) 13
Wolf Kindred (Jensen) 14
Wolf Winter (Ekbäck) 15
The Wolfish Grey (Linderholm) 13
A Woman of Our Time (Linder) 8
Wyndham, John 12

Year Walk 15, 18

Printed in the USA
CPSIA information can be obtained
at www.ICGtesting.com
JSHW021719310723
45679JS00001B/15